· New and Improved ·
Stupid Mac Tricks

LIMITED WARRANTY AND DISCLAIMER OF LIABILITY

ACADEMIC PRESS, INC. ("AP") AND ANYONE ELSE WHO HAS BEEN INVOLVED IN THE CREATION OR PRODUCTION OF THE ACCOMPANYING CODE ("THE PRODUCT") CANNOT AND DO NOT WARRANT THE PERFORMANCE OR RESULTS THAT MAY BE OBTAINED BY USING THE PRODUCT. THE PRODUCT IS SOLD "AS IS" WITHOUT WARRANTY OF ANY KIND (EXCEPT AS HEREAFTER DESCRIBED), EITHER EXPRESSED OR IMPLIED, INCLUDING, BUT NOT LIMITED TO, ANY WARRANTY OF PERFORMANCE OR ANY IMPLIED WARRANTY OF MERCHANTABILITY OR FITNESS FOR ANY PARTICULAR PURPOSE. AP WARRANTS ONLY THAT THE MAGNETIC DISKETTE(S) ON WHICH THE CODE IS RECORDED IS FREE FROM DEFECTS IN MATERIAL AND FAULTY WORKMANSHIP UNDER THE NORMAL USE AND SERVICE FOR A PERIOD OF NINETY (90) DAYS FROM THE DATE THE PRODUCT IS DELIVERED. THE PURCHASER'S SOLE AND EXCLUSIVE REMEDY IN THE EVENT OF A DEFECT IS EXPRESSLY LIMITED TO EITHER REPLACEMENT OF THE DISKETTE(S) OR REFUND OF THE PURCHASE PRICE, AT AP'S SOLE DISCRETION.

IN NO EVENT, WHETHER AS A RESULT OF BREACH OF CONTRACT, WARRANTY OR TORT (INCLUDING NEGLIGENCE), WILL AP OR ANYONE WHO HAS BEEN INVOLVED IN THE CREATION OR PRODUCTION OF THE PRODUCT BE LIABLE TO PURCHASER FOR ANY DAMAGES, INCLUDING ANY LOST PROFITS, LOST SAVINGS OR OTHER INCIDENTAL OR CONSEQUENTIAL DAMAGES ARISING OUT OF THE USE OR INABILITY TO USE THE PRODUCT OR ANY MODIFICATIONS THEREOF, OR DUE TO THE CONTENTS OF THE CODE, EVEN IF AP HAS BEEN ADVISED OF THE POSSIBILITY OF SUCH DAMAGES, OR FOR ANY CLAIM BY ANY OTHER PARTY.

Any request for replacement of a defective diskette must be postage prepaid and must be accompanied by the original defective diskette, your mailing address and telephone number, and proof of date of purchase and purchase price. Send such requests, stating the nature of the problem, to Academic Press Customer Service, 6277 Sea Harbor Drive, Orlando, FL 32887, 1-800-321-5068. APP shall have no obligation to refund the purchase price or to replace a diskette based on claims of defects in the nature or operation of the Product.

Some states do not allow limitation on how long an implied warranty lasts, nor exclusions or limitations of incidental or consequential damage, so the above limitations and exclusions may not apply to you. This Warranty gives you specific legal rights, and you may also have other rights which vary from jurisdiction to jurisdiction.

THE RE-EXPORT OF UNITED STATES ORIGIN SOFTWARE IS SUBJECT TO THE UNITED STATES LAWS UNDER THE EXPORT ADMINISTRATION ACT OF 1969 AS AMENDED. ANY FURTHER SALE OF THE PRODUCT SHALL BE IN COMPLIANCE WITH THE UNITED STATES DEPARTMENT OF COMMERCE ADMINISTRATION REGULATIONS. COMPLIANCE WITH SUCH REGULATIONS IS YOUR RESPONSIBILITY AND NOT THE RESPONSIBILITY OF AP.

· New and Improved ·
Stupid Mac Tricks

Bob LeVitus

AP PROFESSIONAL

Boston   San Diego   New York
London   Sydney   Tokyo   Toronto

This book is printed on acid-free paper. ∞

Copyright © 1995 by Academic Press, Inc.

All rights reserved.
No part of this publication may be reproduced or transmitted in any form or by any means, electronic or mechanical, including photocopy, recording, or any information storage and retrieval system, without permission in writing from the publisher.

All brand names and product names mentioned in
this book are trademarks or registered trademarks
of their respective companies.

AP PROFESSIONAL
1300 Boylston Street, Chestnut Hill, MA 02167

An Imprint of ACADEMIC PRESS, INC.
A Division of HARCOURT BRACE & COMPANY

United Kingdom Edition published by
ACADEMIC PRESS LIMITED
24–28 Oval Road, London NW1 7DX

ISBN 0-12-445578-6

Printed in the United States of America
95 96 97 98   IP   9 8 7 6 5 4 3 2 1

TABLE OF CONTENTS
A Guide to the Delights That Await You

Acknowledgments

Preface
The Moose Is Dead ....*xi*

Introduction
System Requirements and Installation Instructions and Disclaimers (Oh, My!) ....*xiii*

UnderWare
The UnderWare that's Fun to Wear 1

StartupScreen
Startup Screen Will Make 'em Scream! 7

TABLE OF CONTENTS

Critters
Eyeballs & BigFoot Run Rampant on your Desktop 11

Enchanted Menus
Make Your Menus Do Really Weird Stuff 15

EarthQuake
For a Rocking Good Time 19

Shakespeare
Shakespeare in a Toaster? 23

Blood
Blood Drops Keep Falling on My Screen… 29

EyeCon
Eyeballs Everywhere! 33

Belch!
The Really Gross Mac Trick! 37

Melt
A Meltdown for Your Monitor! 41

Subliminal
Brainwashing Made Stupid 45

TappyType
The Macs Are Alive, with the Sound of Typing! 53

Key Lights
The Wacky Treat for Your Keyboard's Lights 57

Bunch o' Icons
A Bevy of Delectable and Delightful Icons
(Plus Some Nifty Desktop Patterns!) 61

Sexist Mac Tricks
Sexplosion, Babe-O-Rama, and Jiggling Jugs 69

> **Sexplosion**
> *It's Not What You Expect…* 71
>
> **Babe-O-Rama**
> *It's DEFINITELY Not What You Expect…* 75
>
> **Jiggling Jugs**
> *It Really Does Show Jiggling Jugs*
> *(But It's Not What You Expect)* 79

Glossary
Daffy-Nitions 83

Acknowledgments

To the programmers who dare to dream them up—
you are the true heroes of *New & Improved Stupid Mac Tricks*.

So first and foremost, extra special thanks to Mike, Chris, and everyone at Bit Jugglers, Inc., for UnderWare Demo, Phil Reed for Startup Screen, Ben Haller for Critters, Fred D. Reed for Enchanted Menus, Marco Carra for EarthQuake, Bob Schumaker for both Shakespeare and Sexplosion, Alex Levi Montalcini for Blood, Michael C. Koss for EyeCon, Andrew Welch/Ambrosia Software, Inc., for Belch!, Gordon A. Acocella for Melt, Evan Gross for Subliminal, Colin Klipsch for TappyType, Rick Kaseguma for Key Lights, Sachiko Oba and George Stolz for their icons and desktop patterns, and last, but not least, Brian Cyr for Babe-O-Rama and Jiggling Jugs.

I'd also like to thank Charles "Chuck" Glaser, my way-cool executive editor, for sharing my vision of doing something really stupid every so often. Thanks, Chuck. Thanks also to everyone else at AP PROFESSIONAL for their help, guidance, and encouragement.

Special thanks to Keith and Steve, and the gang at Addison-Wesley, for graciously allowing us to go forward with this project.

Thanks to my agent, Carol "don't call me Swifty in print" McClendon for another smashing success. You're still awesome.

Thanks to Samuel Adams, The Iron Works, Matthew Sweet, Hootie and the Blowfish, and Power Computing Corporation, each of whom somehow contributed to this whole shebang.

And last but not least, thanks to my family—Lisa, Allison, and Jacob—for putting up with my lengthy stints in the office and all the funny noises. I've missed y'all. I'll be back soon.

PREFACE
The Moose Is Dead

It all began with *Stupid Mac Tricks* back in 1990. I began the preface of that book:

> Thanks for buying this copy of Stupid Mac Tricks. (If you're standing in a book or software store reading this, go directly to the counter and buy it. You'll like it. Trust me.) You'll have as good a time using the tricks I've collected to delight, amuse, and entertain yourself, your friends, and your coworkers as I had putting it together. And that's a real good time.
>
> If you're wondering why a serious, dedicated, and well-known Macintosh journalist such as myself would embark on such a wacky project, all I can say in my defense is, "The Moose made me do it."

It was the Talking Moose I referred to, the most famous trick in the original collection. And now, alas, the Talking Moose is dead. His publisher doesn't answer the phone anymore, and his author (father), Steve Halls, is a successful doctor in Canada these days.

Which brings us to the start of my story. If you're familiar with *Stupid Mac Tricks* or *Son of Stupid Mac Tricks* (both near-impossible to find these days), you know that many of the tricks—including the Moose—are not compatible with System 7 or the new Power Macintoshes.

For years I've been dying to do a new *Stupid* book, with all the tricks System 7.x compatible and PowerPC tested, a book that combined the best of *Stupid Mac Tricks* and *Son of Stupid Mac Tricks* with the coolest new tricks of the past couple of years. But without the Moose, I despaired, it would never happen. I'd never again find a trick goofy enough to lead off my dream book. And as time passed, I felt certain I'd never get *New & Improved Stupid Mac Tricks* off the ground.

Then I saw UnderWare. It was love at first sight—finally, a program so profoundly stupid, so intuitively insipid, so weird, that I could actually see it anchoring *New & Improved Stupid Mac Tricks*. I quickly struck a deal with its publisher to include a demo version that featured its two stupidest modules—Billy Bounce and Rockettes. I even got the publisher to offer you a big discount on the full version. (See page 21.)

The rest, as they say, is history. You hold in your hand the latest, greatest, most state-of-the-art *Stupid* book ever written. So check out UnderWare and the other new tricks, such as EarthQuake, Belch!, and Babe-O-Rama, plus the gorgeous new Icons and Desktop Patterns. And revisit classic Stupid tricks, such as Sexplosion, Melt, Subliminal, and all the others.

And once again I can say with a straight face, Stupid Mac Tricks are the most fun you can have with your Mac on.

Bob LeVitus
Summer 1995

Introduction

System Requirements and Installation Instructions and Disclaimers (Oh, My!)

System Requirements

First, here's what you'll need to use *New & Improved Stupid Mac Tricks*: any Macintosh running Macintosh Operating System version 7.0 or later, a hard disk drive, and a high-density floppy disk drive. A color monitor is recommended but not essential to the enjoyment of most tricks.

Before You Install the Tricks

Some tricks may conflict with other programs you use. In particular, many of the tricks are extensions and control panels and may conflict with other extensions and control panels you already have running on your Macintosh. If this happens to you after installing a trick, merely restart while holding down the Shift key, remove the trick that's causing the problem from your Extensions or Control Panels folder, then restart.

How To Install The Tricks

The New & Improved Stupid Mac Tricks disk contains almost 1600K of fun. I used technology from Aladdin Systems, makers of StuffIt, to compress the files and create an Installer program that would fit on a single high-density floppy disk. So before you can use the tricks, you'll have to decompress them onto your hard disk. It's easy. Here's how:

1. Put the New & Improved Stupid Mac Tricks disk in any floppy disk drive. Double-click the New & Improved Stupid Installer. The Stupid Installer Splash Screen will appear.

2. Click the Continue button. The Stupid Installer dialog box will appear.

3. Click the Install button. The Select Disk dialog box will appear.

4. Click the Switch Disk button until you see the name of your hard disk appear then click the Install button. (See Figure 1.)

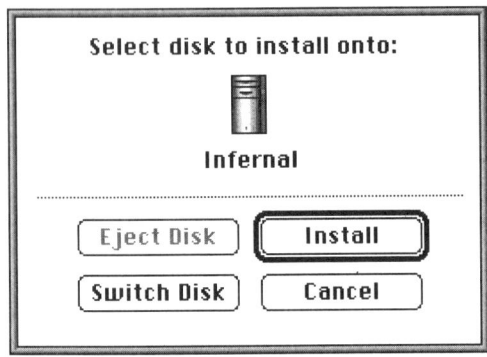

Figure 1: *The Select Disk dialog box. Click Switch Disk until your hard disk's name appears at the top (it's Infernal in this picture).*

A screen with a thermometer showing the progress of the installer will appear. When the thermometer gets to 100%, you'll be told that the installation was successful, and you'll find a folder entitled N & I Stupid Mac Tricks Folder on the hard disk you selected in step 4. The process will take about five minutes or less, depending on the kind of Mac you have.

All of the tricks are now in the N & I Stupid Mac Tricks Folder on your hard disk. Each is described in its own section. Follow the specific directions for each trick, and don't forget that if a folder contains a file called Read Me, you should probably read it before using that particular trick.

Using the Tricks

One more note about using the tricks. Despite my extensive testing, you may experience a crash with a particular trick. If you attempt to use a trick and you experience a crash, bomb, or freeze, try restarting your Mac. If you immediately crash again while restarting, follow these steps:

1. Insert the Disk Tools disk that came with your Mac (or any Startup disk).

2. Restart your Mac. If the Disk Tools disk pops out, push it back in as quickly as you can.

3. Open the System Folder of the Mac you installed the tricks on (most probably your hard disk).

4. Move the trick that initiated the crash out of the Extensions or Control Panels folder (both can be found in your System Folder).

5. Restart your Mac, allowing it to eject the Disk Tools disk.

If a particular trick continually crashes with your system, I encourage you to contact the author of the trick directly. Most of the tricks come with documentation or help files that tell you how to get in touch with the authors.

Disclaimer

The author makes no claims about the performance of the tricks on the New & Improved Stupid Mac Tricks disk. I have tested each one on a variety of Macs, and all seem to work as advertised in my (albeit) limited testing. I feel relatively certain that they are not going to do any damage to your Mac (like trash your hard disk or burn up your motherboard). However, I make no guarantees—use them at your own risk.

I'm a firm believer in backing up your hard disk. I strongly recommend that there be a backup available before you try these tricks on yourself or others. If you don't have one, I suggest that you create one now, just in case.

Some tricks may conflict with other programs you use. There was no way I could test every possible combination of hardware and software. I apologize if something doesn't work on your particular setup, but I cannot be held responsible.

UNDERWARE

The UnderWare that's Fun to Wear

WHAT UNDERWARE DEMO DOES

UnderWare is perhaps the stupidest program ever invented, a tad stupider than even the old and beloved Talking Moose. You may be tempted to think of UnderWare as a mere screen saver, but UnderWare is more fun than a barrel of screen savers. It's much more than a screen saver—it's also a desktop animator and a collection of beautiful desktop patterns. (See page 81 for more about Desktop Patterns.) Best of all, the demo version of UnderWare included with this book is absolutely free!

HOW TO USE UNDERWARE

UnderWare comes with its own Installer program that installs the UnderWare files in their proper places automatically. Open the UnderWare folder, then double-click the UnderWare™ Installer icon. Click Continue, then click Install, then click Yes when asked if it's OK to restart your computer once the installation is complete. Now kick back for a moment and let the Installer do its thing. When it's done, click the Restart button.

(If you care about such things, the Installer placed the UnderWare icon in your Control Panels folder and the UnderWare Files folder in your Preferences folder.)

That's it! UnderWare Demo is installed! If you do nothing else, you'll soon notice a character named Billy trapped inside your monitor. (See Figure 2.)

Figure 2: *It's Billy, trapped inside your monitor for eternity.*

He'll bounce off the sides of your screen, conk his head on the glass, and even carom off your desktop icons and any open windows. That's UnderWare's Desktop Animation feature in action at its most bizarre.

(*Note:* I would never be so bold as to suggest which Billy I think that is.... Not even if you drag me to the pearly GATES. Or threaten to make my MICROcomputer SOFTware crash. Or even throw me out WINDOWS in '95. I EXCEL at keeping secrets—you won't get a WORD out of me.)

But that is not all—oh, no, that is not all.... If you leave your Mac idle for five minutes, you'll see another of UnderWare's kooky features—its animated screen saver. You'll know it when you see it: The icons on your desktop will sprout legs, form a chorus line, and dance around the screen. (See Figure 3.)

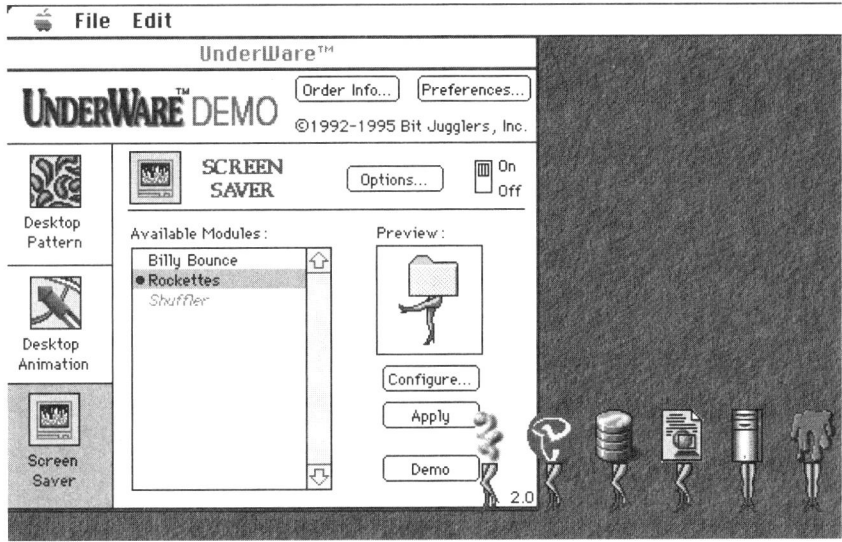

Figure 3: *The Rockettes module makes your icons get up and dance to a catchy tune!*

Open UnderWare in your Control Panels folder to configure your Desktop Animation and Screen Saver modules or to change your desktop pattern. To configure the Desktop Animation or Screen Saver modules, click the appropriate item on the left side of the UnderWare Demo control panel, then click the Configure button. A window similar to the one shown in Figure 4 will appear.

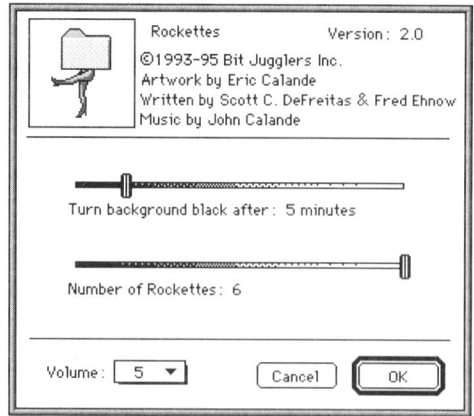

Figure 4: *Both the Desktop Animation and Screen Saver modules can be configured to work just the way you like them.*

Make your adjustments, click OK, and continue to enjoy the stupidity of your UnderWare Demo.

To change desktop patterns, first click the Desktop Pattern button on the left side of the screen. (See Figure 5.)

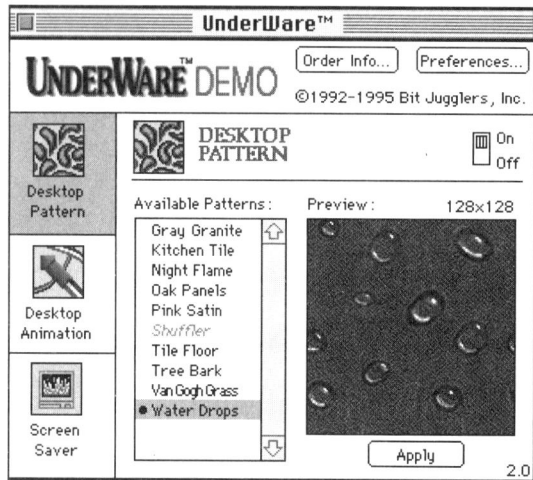

Figure 5: *To change your desktop pattern, click Desktop Pattern on the left, then choose and apply a pattern.*

To customize UnderWare even further, be sure and check out the Options button in both the Desktop Animation and Screen Saver modules, and the Preference button.

Suggestions for Using UnderWare Demo

Well, I like UnderWare so much, I use it on my computer all the time! People really get a kick out of it when they see it. It's also quite unsettling to install on someone else's machine. As one of my daughter's favorite songs says, "It's just so fun!"

UnderWare Demo: Fine Print

UnderWare Demo © 1992–1995 Bit Jugglers, Inc.

Liner Notes

UnderWare Demo is a new Stupid trick. It's great, but it is only the demo! The full commercial version of UnderWare has more than 35 animated modules, including gorillas, dinosaurs, gophers, landscapes, dragons, ballerinas, cats and dogs, babies, dancing icons, as well as more than 120 professionally designed desktop patterns. (UnderWare is also the only commercial screen saver engine that is Power Macintosh native!)

If you like the demo, you'll love the full version. If you want a copy of your very own, you'll get it for the extra-special "I-bought-a-copy-*New-&-Improved-Stupid-Mac-Tricks*-price" of just $19.95. Give Bit Jugglers a call at (800) 454-4449, send them a fax at (415) 968-5358, or send them e-mail at orders@bitjugglers.com.

 STARTUPSCREEN

Startup Screen Will Make 'em Scream!

WHAT STARTUPSCREEN DOES

StartupScreen replaces the "Welcome to Macintosh" or "Mac OS" (System 7.5.1 and later) message you ordinarily see when you first start your Mac. This message is a little less upbeat. It asks whether you want to erase the ROMs, warns you that the operation is not reversible, and offers you only one choice: "I guess so." (See Figure 6.)

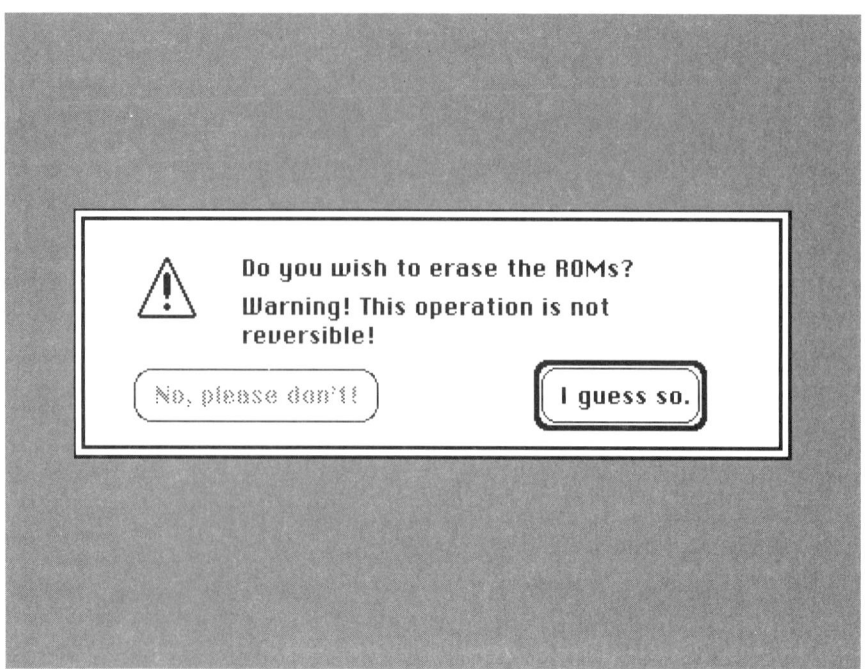

Figure 6: *StartupScreen replaces the cheerful "Welcome to Macintosh" with something a little less comforting.*

How to Use StartupScreen

Just drag the file StartupScreen onto the System Folder. The next time the computer is restarted, instead of seeing "Welcome to Macintosh," you'll see the screen shown in Figure 6.

Don't worry. It's not a real dialog box, and your ROMs won't be erased. In fact, the computer won't let you click the button; it just shows this screen for a few seconds during the startup process.

To return to the old "Welcome to Macintosh" startup screen, simply remove the StartupScreen file from your System Folder.

Suggestions for Using StartupScreen

I keep StartupScreen installed on my Mac at all times. That way, someone who comes along and decides to start my computer up is in for a shocking surprise. It's also fun to drop a copy in someone else's System Folder; I suggest trying this only on people with well-developed senses of humor.

StartupScreen is a special feature of the Macintosh Operating System, now known officially as "Mac OS." It's easy to create one yourself; all you need is an application capable of saving a file in the StartupScreen format. Many paint programs have this capability, including Photoshop, SuperPaint, UltraPaint, PixelPaint, Studio 8, and MacPaint 2.0. Others may as well. If you're not sure, refer to your manual.

Once you've created a picture using one of these programs, you need to save it in the StartupScreen format and name it StartupScreen. To make it replace the Welcome to Macintosh message, all you have to do is drop it into your System Folder.

You can have lots of fun creating other startup screens for yourself or your friends.

Startup Screen: Fine Print

StartupScreen © 1990 by Phil Reed. FreeWare.

Liner Notes

StartupScreen is a Stupid Classic from *Stupid Mac Tricks*. I updated this version a little using Adobe Photoshop, replacing the old 1-bit gray background with real gray, which makes the effect more realistic on color monitors (which were still a rarity when the original *Stupid Mac Tricks* was published).

Still, it was Phil Reed's idea. And I still think it's hysterical.

👀 👣 CRITTERS

Eyeballs & BigFoot Run Rampant on Your Desktop...

WHAT CRITTERS DOES

Feeling lonesome? Critters will keep you and your Mac company. Critters is Eyeballs, an extension that installs goo-goo eyes in your menu bar, and BigFoot, an extension that puts a pair of walking footprints on your desktop. (See Figure 7.)

Figure 7 *Critters puts Eyeballs in your menu bar and BigFoot on your desktop. This picture doesn't do them justice—they're much cuter in real life when they're moving to and fro!*

These Critters are well behaved, don't eat much, and are very (user?) friendly. They're also terminally cute.

How to Use Critters

Critters is a pair of extensions, Eyeballs and BigFoot. To activate them, open the Critters folder and drag the Eyeballs and BigFoot icons onto your System Folder. Under System 7 you'll see a dialog confirming that you want to put them in the Extensions folder. Click OK. Now restart your Mac.

The two extensions—Eyeballs and BigFoot—are independent of each other; you can use one, the other, or both. As you might expect, Eyeballs puts the eyes in your menu bar, and BigFoot puts the walking footprints on your desktop. Notice how the Eyeballs follow the pointer/cursor when you move the mouse? Cool, eh?

Suggestions for Using Critters

Critters are friendly fellows and can be installed on your own Mac to keep you company and amuse your friends and coworkers. Or drop them into the System Folder of a friend's or coworker's Mac so someone else can be kept company and amused.

If you want to heighten the surprise, and divert suspicion from yourself (as the perpetrator), try copying both extensions into someone's System Folder, but don't restart the person's Mac. Since extensions don't become active until the Mac is restarted, the Critters will sit there, inert, until your unknowing victim restarts his or her Mac and then gets an entertaining surprise.

Critters: The Fine Print

Critters by Stick Software, c/o Ben Haller, 32 Deer Haven Drive, Ithaca, NY 14850. FreeWare.

LINER NOTES

Critters is a Stupid Classic from *Son of Stupid Mac Tricks*.

Critters is the work of master programmer Ben Haller, the author of Solarian II, one of the greatest shareware Macintosh games ever created. For a copy of Solarian II, a Mac video game that requires 256 colors, send $25 and a self-addressed stamped envelope to Stick Software, c/o Ben Haller, 32 Deer Haven Drive, Ithaca, NY 14850.

Enchanted Menus

Make Your Menus Do Some Really Weird Stuff...

What Enchanted Menus Does

Enchanted Menus makes every menu appear at a random place on your screen—somewhere other than where it should appear. It's harmless but extremely disorienting. (See Figure 8.)

How to Use Enchanted Menus

Enchanted Menus is an extension. Drag the Enchanted Menus icon onto the System Folder icon, click OK when it tells you it's going to put it in the Extensions folder, then restart your Mac to enable Enchanted Menus. Remove it from the Extensions folder (*hint:* it's inside your System Folder) and restart to disable it. That's all there is to it.

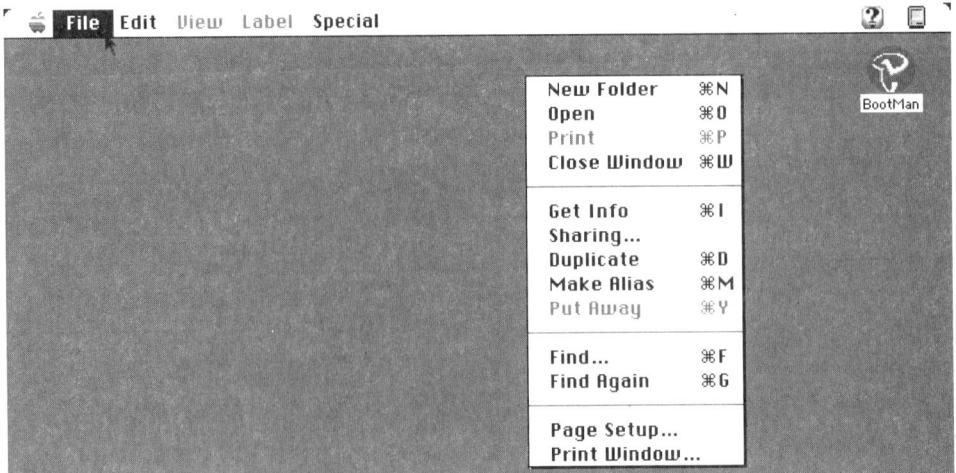

Figure 8: *Enchanted Menus causes your menus to pop up in unexpected locations.*

SUGGESTIONS FOR USING ENCHANTED MENUS

Enchanted Menus is one of the stupid tricks that is fun only once on your own Mac. But it's always a kick to install it on somebody else's machine and watch his or her confused and puzzled look. To do so, copy Enchanted Menus into the System Folder of that person's startup disk and restart the Mac. (After you've had your fun, don't forget to remove it!)

Incidentally, menus that have been "enchanted" work perfectly. They just look really strange.

ENCHANTED MENUS: FINE PRINT

Enchanted Menus © 1987–90 by IMI Software. Written by Fred D. Reed. FreeWare.

LINER NOTES

Enchanted Menus is a Stupid Classic from *Stupid Mac Tricks*. It's reprised here 'cause it's just so plain stupid and it's so confounding to put on a friend's (or enemy's) Mac.

# EARTHQUAKE

For a Rocking Good Time...

WHAT EARTHQUAKE DOES

EarthQuake, like its namesake, shakes your Mac's screen to and fro while playing an ominous rumbling sound through your speaker. Not much chance of mistaking this cheesy EarthQuake for the real thing. Still, it can be quite unsettling, especially if you've been through a real shaker (I've been in two major ones and hope to never experience one again).

HOW TO USE EARTHQUAKE

EarthQuake is a control panel. Drag the EarthQuake 1.0 icon onto the System Folder icon, click OK when it tells you it's going to put it in the Control Panels folder, then restart your Mac to enable EarthQuake. Remove it from the Control Panels folder (*hint:* it's inside your System Folder) and restart your Mac to disable it. Piece of cake for a by-now-experienced Mac Trickster such as yourself.

Once you've restarted, EarthQuake will be enabled. If you do nothing more, sometime in the next 30 minutes your Mac will shake and growl for a while. The duration of each quake is strictly random.

The length of time between EarthQuakes, however, is configurable, as is the On/Off key. To adjust either item, open the EarthQuake 1.0 control panel. (See Figure 9.) To do that, select Control Panels from the Apple menu and then double-click the EarthQuake 1.0 icon.

Figure 9: *The EarthQuake control panel lets you adjust the time between temblors and choose the On/Off keys.*

The time delay can be any whole number between 1 and 60, but it isn't 100% accurate—a small element of randomness is thrown in just for fun. So a time delay of 30 might mean 30 minutes or 26 minutes or even 33 minutes. The default (the setting it uses when you first install it) is 30 minutes.

The On/Off key lets you turn EarthQuake on and off from the keyboard, without a bothersome trip to the control panel. The default setting is Command-Option-Return. To change it, click the Set Keys button, then press the keys you want to be your new On/Off keys.

Suggestions for Using EarthQuake

This is a really good one to put on your best friend's (or your worst enemy's) Mac. It's subtle. If you set the time delay to 60 minutes, it could be hours before the person experiences a shaker and is surprised. But be careful—your friend or enemy could have a copy of *Cruel and Unusual Mac Tricks* (coming soon)!

EarthQuake: Fine Print

EarthQuake 1.0 by Marco Carra. ShareWare.

EarthQuake can be distributed freely, but it cannot be altered in any way or sold, either as an individual program or as part of a package, without written permission.

You may try it free for 30 days. If after this trial period you decide to keep EarthQuake, please send $5 to the following address. California residents, add sales tax. Paying the registration fee entitles you to receive discounts on future upgrades.

SLIMYFROG SOFTWARE
979 Golf Course Drive #213
Rohnert Park, CA 94928

Liner Notes

EarthQuake is a new Stupid Mac Trick, although it's been floating around the Internet for about a year. In it Marco Carra has created a perfectly stupid trick that's both devious and silly at the same time. That's not easy.

Hats off to you, Marco!

SHAKESPEARE

Shakespeare in a Toaster?

WHAT SHAKESPEARE DOES

Billed as "Shakespeare in a Toaster," Shakespeare is a program that generates sonnets, 14-line poems with traditional rules of structure and rhyme. Although this Shakespeare's sonnets rarely make sense, they are usually amusing and, occasionally, hilarious.

How To Use Shakespeare

Shakespeare is an application—a program. Just double-click its icon to start it. When you launch Shakespeare, the first thing you'll see is a credit screen with a picture of Shakespeare himself. Click the OK button, and you'll see the Help Window. The Help Window pretty much tells you everything you need to know to get Shakespeare to write a sonnet for you. (See Figure 10.)

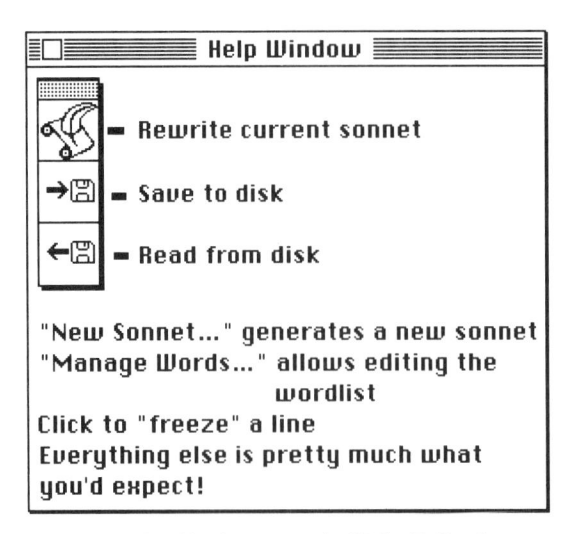

```
╔════════════ Help Window ════════════╗
║ ▄                                    ║
║ ▓                                    ║
║ ⌐┐ - Rewrite current sonnet          ║
║                                      ║
║ →💾 - Save to disk                    ║
║                                      ║
║ ←💾 - Read from disk                  ║
║                                      ║
║ "New Sonnet..." generates a new sonnet║
║ "Manage Words..." allows editing the ║
║                      wordlist        ║
║ Click to "freeze" a line             ║
║ Everything else is pretty much what  ║
║ you'd expect!                        ║
╚══════════════════════════════════════╝
```

Figure 10: *Shakespeare's Help Window appears when you launch the program and is always available in the Apple menu.*

To generate a new sonnet, choose New Sonnet from the File menu (be patient—it takes a while). Once you've created a sonnet, you can use the Rewrite Current Sonnet button (the top button in the tool palette) to replace all or part of your poem. If there are lines you want to retain, click on them once to "freeze" them. Frozen lines appear in italic type. (See Figure 11.)

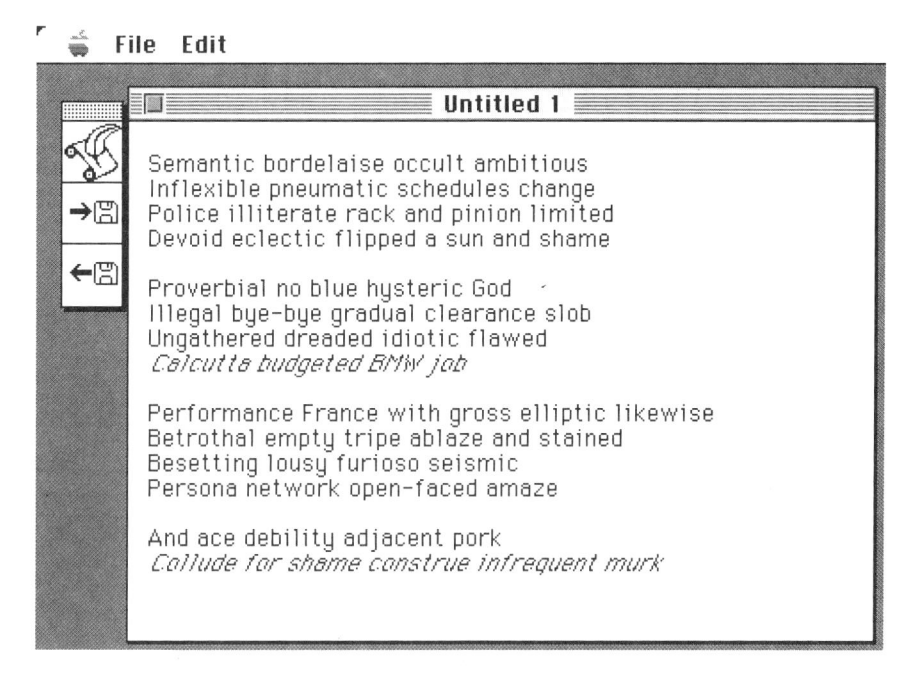

```
 ╔ File  Edit
┌─────────────────────────────────────────┐
│ ▣          Untitled 1                   │
│   Semantic bordelaise occult ambitious  │
│   Inflexible pneumatic schedules change │
│   Police illiterate rack and pinion limited │
│   Devoid eclectic flipped a sun and shame │
│                                         │
│   Proverbial no blue hysteric God       │
│   Illegal bye-bye gradual clearance slob│
│   Ungathered dreaded idiotic flawed     │
│   Calcutta budgeted BMW job             │
│                                         │
│   Performance France with gross elliptic likewise │
│   Betrothal empty tripe ablaze and stained │
│   Besetting lousy furioso seismic       │
│   Persona network open-faced amaze      │
│                                         │
│   And ace debility adjacent pork        │
│   Collude for shame construe infrequent murk │
└─────────────────────────────────────────┘
```

Figure 11: *Shakespeare's main window; lines in italic are frozen.*

If you were to click the Rewrite Current Sonnet (top) button now, all the lines except the two that begin "Calcutta" and "Collude" would be replaced with new lines.

The other two buttons in the palette allow you to save a sonnet to disk as a text file or to reopen a sonnet that you saved previously. The Save and Open commands in the File menu mimic the functions of these two buttons.

When you save a sonnet, it can be opened again with Shakespeare, any text editor (for example, SimpleText or TeachText), or a word processor. You can also print your sonnet by using the Print Sonnet command in the File menu, or, if you want to print it in your choice of fonts, you can save your sonnet to disk and then open, format, and print it using your word processor.

You can edit Shakespeare's word list and add your own words to its vocabulary, but it's not particularly intuitive and will require quite a bit of trial and error. If you're brave enough to give it a try, choose Manage Words (Command-M) from the Edit menu. This opens the

Manage Wordlist window. To add a word, type it into the Word field; then make selections about how the word sounds from the "Scans like," "Vowel type," and "Consonant" pop-up menus. To invoke these pop-up menus, click to the right of their names, as shown in Figure 12. You'll have to experiment to get your words to work just right; I still haven't quite gotten the hang of it.

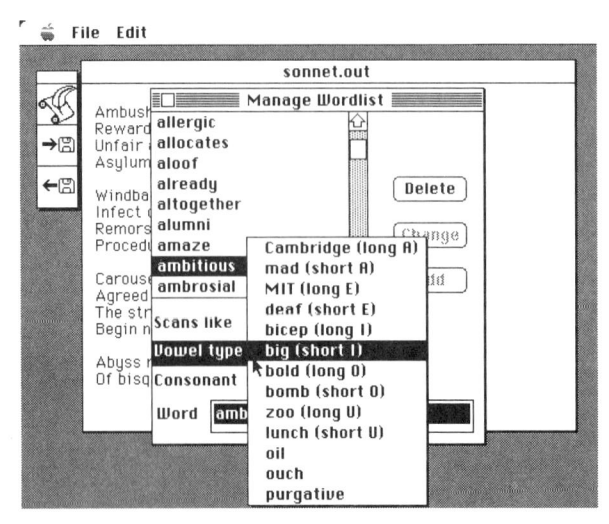

Figure 12: *Managing Shakespeare's words is not for the faint of heart, but can be rewarding and sort of fun.*

SUGGESTIONS FOR USING SHAKESPEARE

Unlike other stupid tricks, Shakespeare can't easily be inflicted on the unsuspecting. Or can it? You can always create a sonnet and send it to a loved one. Don't sign it. The recipient will go crazy trying to figure out who the secret admirer with the penchant for poetry is.

SHAKESPEARE: THE FINE PRINT

Shakespeare Mac Version © 1991 Bob Schumaker. HappiWare—if you like it, smile!

LINER NOTES

> Shakespeare is a Stupid Classic from *Son of Stupid Mac Tricks*. It's included again in this collection because it's about as stupid as a trick can get.
>
> Don't believe me? Try reading one of Shakespeare's sonnets aloud without cracking up.

Blood

Blood Drops Keep Falling on My Screen...

What Blood Does

Blood is a control panel that spatters realistic-looking blood drops on your screen. (See Figure 13.) In the author's own words, it's "absolutely useless."

Still, it has a certain stupid appeal, and I thought it should be included.

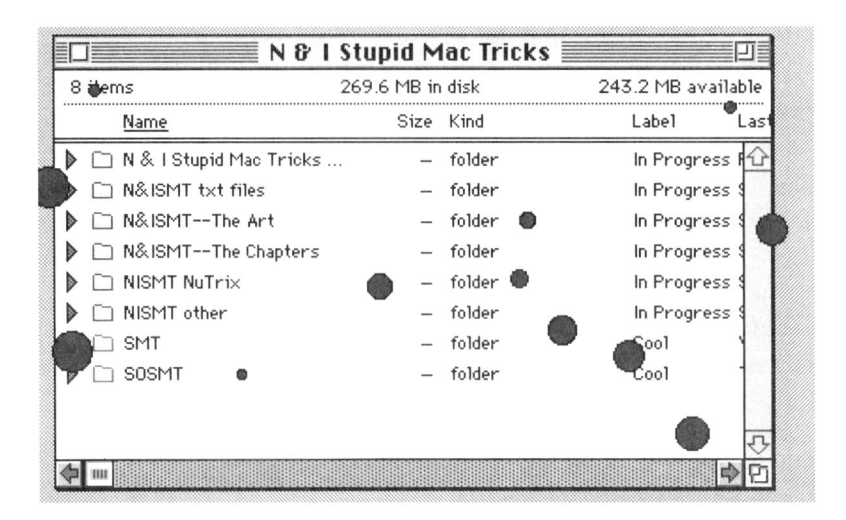

Figure 13: *A blood-spattered window. This screen shot doesn't do the blood drops justice; on a color monitor, the gore is very, very red.*

How To Use Blood

To activate the Blood control panel, open the Blood folder, then drag the Blood icon onto your System Folder. You'll see the old "Control panels need to be stored in the Control Panels folder…" dialog box. Click OK, then restart your Mac.

Once you've restarted, Blood will be turned on and will spatter your screen with blood drops without any further interaction on your part. The drops float over everything—windows, icons, etc. To move them, merely click and drag. To remove them, hold down the Option key and click 'em.

The droplets are configurable; if you want to change the drop size or number of drops, use the Blood control panel. (See Figure 14.) To do so, select Control Panels from the Apple menu and then double-click the Blood icon.

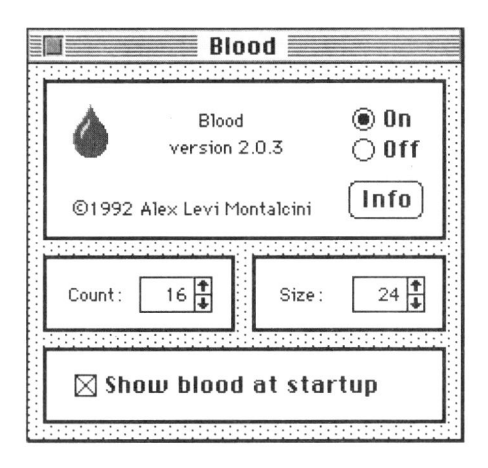

Figure 14: *Specify how big and how many drops in the Blood control panel. The "Show blood at startup" checkbox splashes blood on your screen during the "march of extensions and control panels" most people see at startup.*

Suggestions for Using Blood

Use your imagination. If you're the macabre type, run it on your own Mac every day.

Or, for a bigger thrill, put it on a friend's or coworker's machine. Then stroll up and accuse him or her of wounding a poor innocent Macintosh. "What on earth did you DO to it? It's bleeding all over the place!!!"

Blood: Fine Print

Blood © 1992 Alex Levi Montalcini. FreeWare.

Liner Notes

Although Blood is a new Stupid Mac Trick, it's been popular on the Internet and online services for years. Its talented author, Alessandro Levi Montalcini, has written must-have shareware programs, such as KeyQuencer and PowerPCheck. If you have Internet access, the latest versions of all his stuff are always available via anonymous ftp at: //ftp.alpcom.it/software/mac/LMontalcini.

EyeCon
Eyeballs Everywhere!

What EyeCon Does

EyeCon is a program that puts goo-goo-googly eyes on your screen. These desktop eyeballs, like Critters' menu-bar Eyeballs, follow your cursor when it moves. (See Figure 15.)

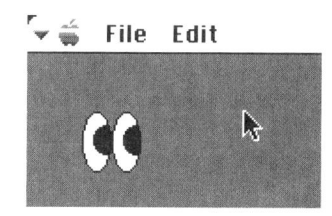

Figure 15: *When you launch EyeCon, you'll see a single pair of googly eyes.*

How To Use EyeCon

EyeCon is an application. Just double-click its icon and it will start. The eyes are also adjustable—you can stretch them or move them by clicking and dragging. Click near the middle of the eyes to move them; click near an edge to reshape.

The eyes are most enjoyable. They use only 150K of RAM and can be left running all the time. If you have enough RAM, you may find that you like them enough to waste the 150K you'll need to keep them running all the time.

Suggestions for Using EyeCon

There are several things you can do with EyeCon, several really stupid things. You can stretch them, you can fill your screen with dozens of them, you can gaze longingly into them. The possibilities are endless!

Let's start by learning how to change the size of the eyes (Figures 16, 17, and 18):

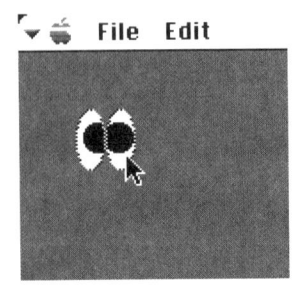

Figure 16: *To resize a pair of eyes, first click in the lower-right part of the right eyeball.*

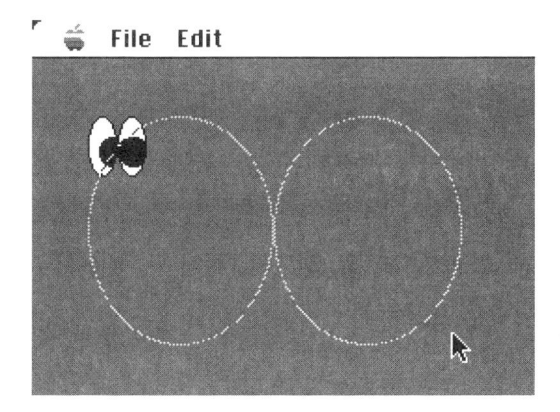

Figure 17: *Then, while continuing to hold down the mouse button, drag to the right and down.*

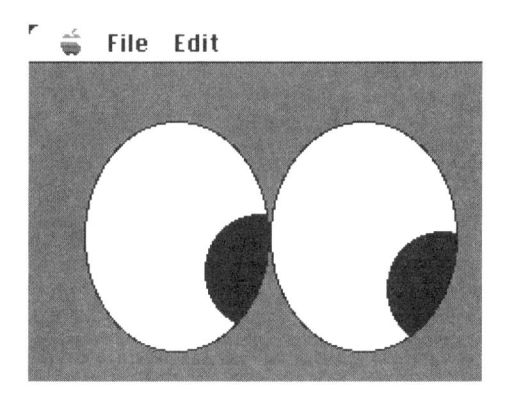

Figure 18: *Finally, release the mouse button and there they are—bigger, better, googlier eyes.*

To move a pair of eyes around onscreen, click close to the middle, where the eyeballs meet, then drag.

Another fun thing to do with EyeCon is create multiple sets of eyes onscreen. It's as easy as selecting New from the File menu. You can have as many as you like. (See Figure 19.)

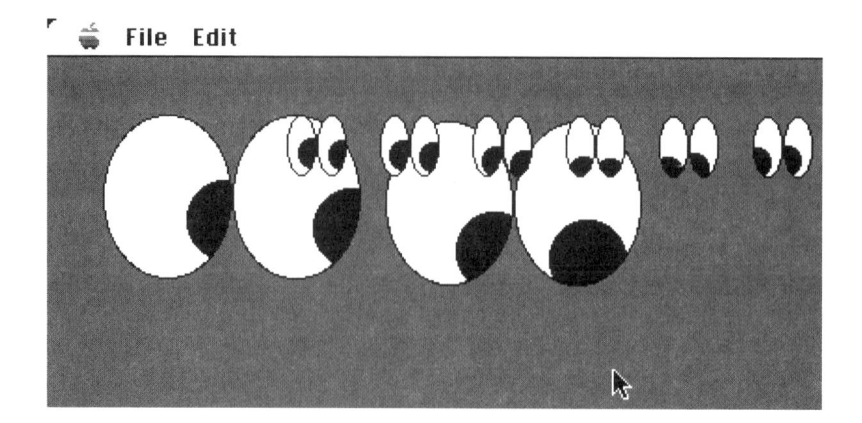

Figure 19: *Use the File menu's New command (or its shortcut, Command-N) to create a screenful of staring eyeballs.*

If you're going to put EyeCon on a friend's machine, you can stash EyeCon in his/her Startup Items folder (inside the System Folder). Then EyeCon will run automatically every time the Mac is turned on.

By the way, the eyes will follow your cursor even if EyeCon is not the active application. (This is another way of saying that EyeCon runs beautifully in the background.)

EYECON: FINE PRINT

EyeCon ©1989 by Michael C. Koss. FreeWare.

LINER NOTES

> EyeCon is a Stupid Classic from *Stupid Mac Tricks*. Everyone loves the EyeBalls. They're one of the few tricks people keep around for more than a few minutes. So they're back. And, if I do say so myself, they're better than ever.

BELCH!
The Really Gross Mac Trick!

WHAT BELCH! DOES

Belch! is extremely annoying. It causes the Macintosh it's installed on to emit a juicy burp every few minutes. Worse, the frequency of the burping seems to increase over time until it's belting out three or four big ones in a row, every 10 seconds or so. Belch! takes the prize — with ease — for being the grossest Mac trick in this collection.

HOW TO USE BELCH!

Belch! is an extension. Drag the Belch! icon onto the System Folder icon, click OK when it tells you it's going to put it in the Extensions folder, then restart your Mac to enable Belch! Remove it from the Extensions folder (*hint:* it's inside your System Folder) and restart to disable it. That's all there is to it.

Suggestions for Using Belch!

The way I see it, there are two ways to use Belch!

1. Install it on your own Mac. When someone else hears the juicy burp, wax poetic about how human computers have become, then say this is the last time you're letting your Mac drink beer at lunch.

2. Install it on some poor unsuspecting victim's Mac. Be careful, though—he or she may have a copy of my *Really Vengeful Mac Tricks* (coming soon) and things could get messy.

I have to tell you, Belch! wears thin real quick. I predict it'll last about no more than an hour on your Mac, if that long. Still, you have to admit, it's a pretty stupid (if a little gross) Mac trick. (It lasted less than 15 minutes on my machine.)

Belch!: Fine Print

Belch! is by Andrew Welch/Ambrosia Software, Inc. FreeWare.

Liner Notes

Although Belch! is new to the *Stupid* books, it has been around (and been quite popular) for a while.

Belch! extends a stupid tradition of really gross Mac tricks. It all started with the wildly popular MacBarf, which first appeared in *Stupid Mac Tricks*. MacBarf, for those who've forgotten, erupted a gut-wrenching, vile, vomiting sound whenever you ejected a disk. It was truly disgusting. I had planned to reprise it in this book.

Unfortunately, MacBarf didn't work reliably on my Mac, and I didn't have time to track down the problem or ask Bob Schumaker to rewrite MacBarf yet another time. So MacBarf bit the dust and I was heartbroken without a really gross Mac trick for this collection.

Then it came to me... Andrew Welch's masterwork, Belch! Of course. What could be grosser? Belch! has been around for a couple of years and has no known problems. So special thanks to Andrew and Ambrosia, who permitted me to include Belch! in this collection on very short notice.

So indulge me for a second and allow me to plug their other fine products. They do so much more than burp. They've created fine shareware and freeware programs, such as Easy Envelopes Plus, Big Cheese Key, Bomb Shelter, and Color Switch. They also publish awesome shareware games, such as Chiral and Maelstrom. You'll find all their stuff in the Ambrosia software forum on America Online. It's well worth checking out.

MELT

A Meltdown for Your Monitor!

WHAT MELT DOES

Melt is a desk accessory. Select it from the Apple menu and experience a very unsettling (but totally harmless) melting effect on your screen.

HOW TO USE MELT

Install Melt by dragging its icon onto your System Folder's icon. Your Mac will ask if it's OK to put it in your Apple Menu Items folder.

Once you've installed it, it's easy to use. Just pull down the Apple menu and select Melt. Now sit back and enjoy the show. (See Figures 20, 21, and 22.) Clicking anywhere on the screen stops the melting effect and returns things to normal.

By the way, after you've installed it, you can move it from the Apple Menu Items folder to any folder on your hard disk.

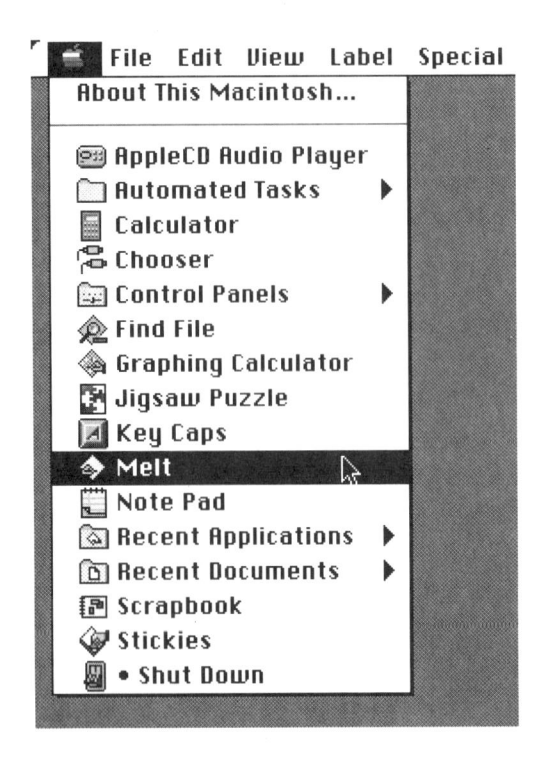

Figure 20: *The fun starts when you choose Melt from the Apple menu.*

Figure 21: *Suddenly your screen begins to melt before your very eyes!*

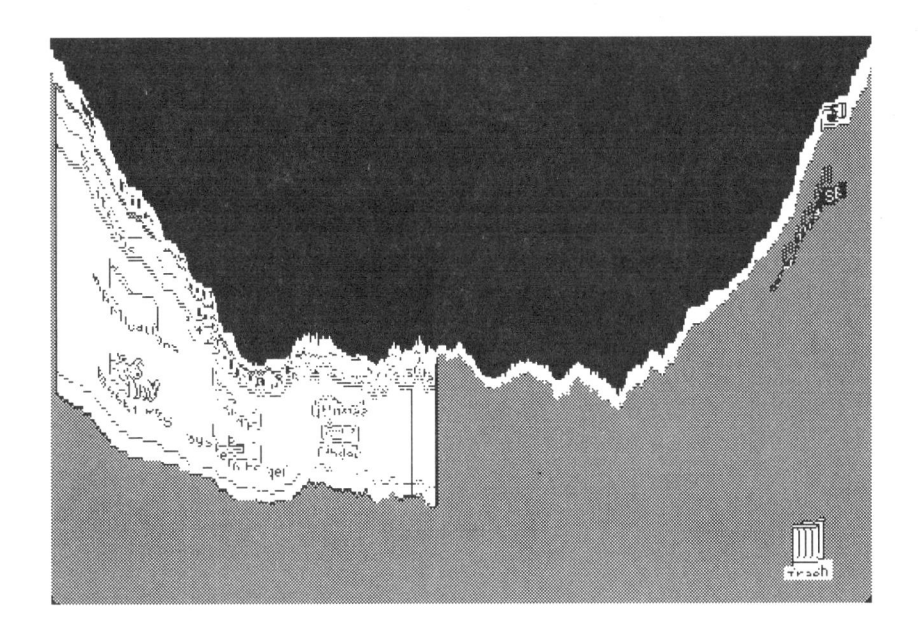

Figure 22: *Until a complete meltdown occurs.*

Suggestions for Using Melt

There are several ways to get more mileage out of Melt. One of my favorites is to get a friend or coworker to come over to your Mac to look at something he or she knows you've spent long hours on, provide a distraction, and then, while the person is looking elsewhere, select Melt from the Apple menu. When your screen starts to melt, shriek, gasp, look appalled, and make accusations of sabotage. If you have a macro program like QuicKeys, Tempo, or AppleScript, you can start Melt with a single keystroke, making it even more effective.

This trick is also effective when performed on someone else's Mac. First, install Melt without letting the person know that you've done so. Then, when something important is on the screen, distract the person

and start Melt by either selecting it from the Apple menu or using a predefined macro. Your victim will freak out. Before you're killed, click anywhere to restore things to normal.

For a final thrill, try stashing a copy of Melt in someone's Startup Items or Shutdown Items folder, both found inside the System Folder. This will cause a meltdown when the person starts up or shuts down the Mac. (It would probably be prudent to explain to your victim what you've done, as well as how to undo it, after you've had your thrill.)

Melt: Fine Print

Melt © 1989–1990 by Gordon A. Acocella. (CompuServe: 73467,1411, GEnie: G.Acocella). FreeWare.

Liner Notes

> Melt is a Stupid Classic from *Stupid Mac Tricks*. It is still among my favorite tricks, and one of the most unsettling to those not in on its secret… (i.e. it's not real).

SUBLIMINAL
Brainwashing Made Stupid

WHAT SUBLIMINAL DOES

According to my dictionary, subliminal (the word) means "designed to act on the mind at a subconscious level." Subliminal (the program) does just that—it sends messages designed to act on the mind at a subconscious level.

It's a do-it-yourself subliminal message kit, useful for influencing yourself or others, most notably spousal units and bosses. (See Figure 23.) You have total control: how often messages appear, how long they appear for, and even what the messages say.

I don't know if it really works. I rather doubt it. You see, it's not really subliminal. Even its shortest display time (one second) is long enough to recognize and read the message (as long as the message is short or you're a fast reader). Truly subliminal messages would appear for fractions of a second, but they wouldn't be as silly or annoying.

There are lots of ways to use Subliminal—as reminders to yourself, as a humorous reminder to your spouse or boss, or even to amuse your kids.

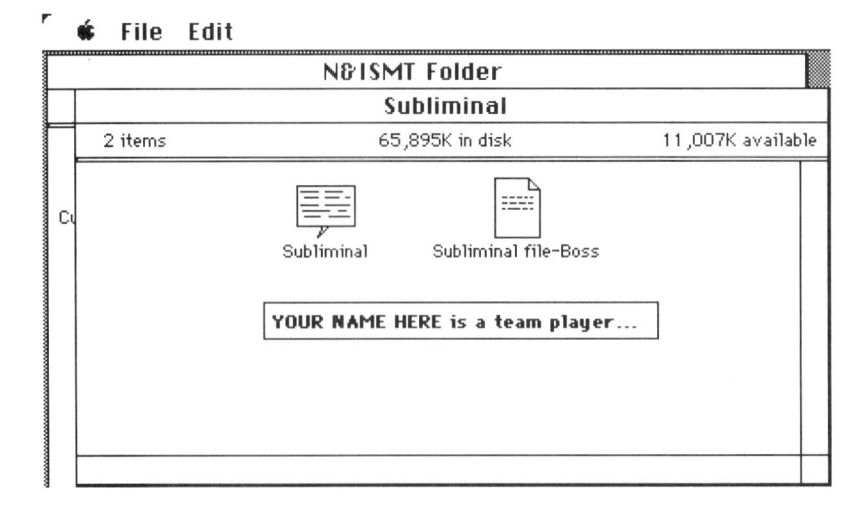

Figure 23: *You think you deserve a raise? Convince your boss by slapping a copy of Subliminal on his or her Mac.*

How To Use Subliminal

Subliminal is a control panel. To activate it, move the Subliminal icon onto your System Folder. You'll see the old "Control panels need to be stored in the Control Panels folder..." dialog box. Click OK, then restart your Mac.

Subliminal will automatically be placed in the Control Panels folder within your System Folder. To use Subliminal, open the Control Panels folder (it's in the System Folder), then open Subliminal. (See Figure 24.)

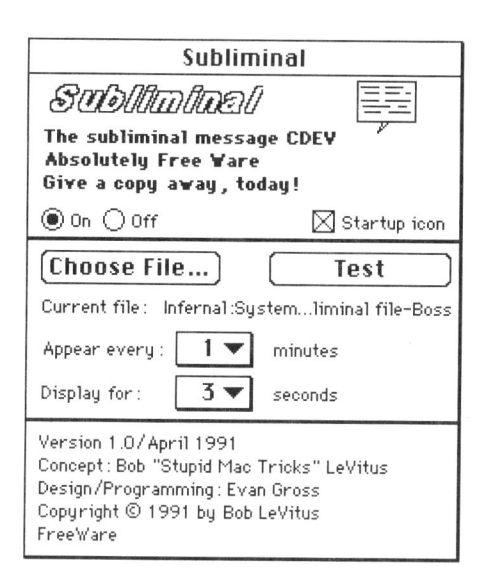

Figure 24: *Subliminal has an easy-to-use interface. Just choose a file and then select values for the "Appear every" and "Display for" fields.*

To select a message file, click the Choose File button, and a standard Open File dialog box will appear. Navigate to the Subliminal folder (it's in the N & I Stupid Mac Tricks folder) and open one of the Subliminal files, either Boss or Self.

Now click the Test button. You should see a message appear somewhere on screen. The messages will continue to pop up at two-second intervals until you click the mouse while a message is on screen.

Subliminal has two other controls: "Appear every" sets the frequency with which messages appear; "Display for" sets the length of time a message stays on screen. Both work the same way, using pop-up menus. To change either one, click on the number in the box and drag up or down until your choice is selected; then release the mouse button. (See Figure 25.)

Figure 25: *To change the value for either pop-up menu, click on the number, drag until your choice is selected, and then release the mouse button.*

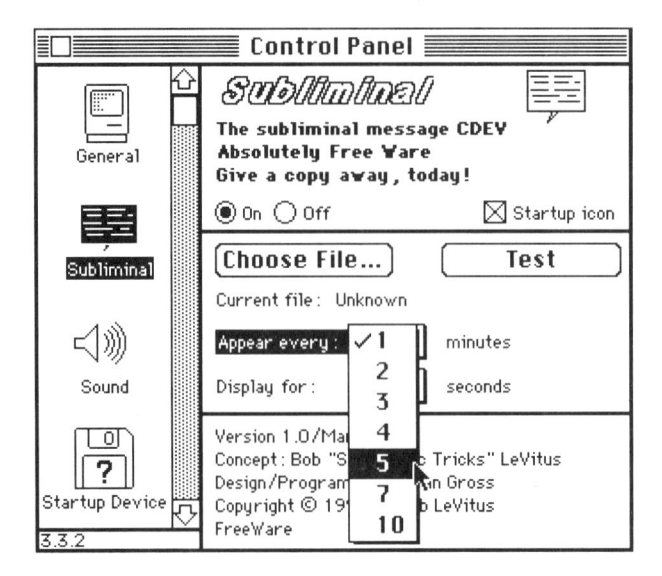

The message files that Subliminal uses are plain text files. You can create and edit files for Subliminal with any word processor that lets you save in "text" format, which is sometimes called "ASCII" or "plain text." Apple's TeachText or SimpleText, the text reading and editing programs that come with every Mac, can also be used to create and edit files for Subliminal. (See Figure 26.)

TeachText saves files in the text format automatically, so if you're not sure how to create a text file with your word processor, use Teach-Text.

There are only two things you need to know to create or change Subliminal files:

1. The file must be saved in text format.

2. Each message must end in a carriage return.

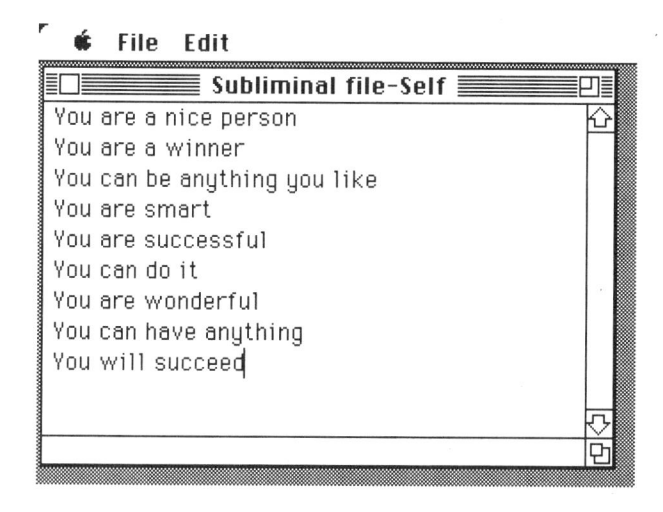

```
 ▄ File  Edit
┌─────────────────────────────────────┐
│ ▭▬▬▬▬▬▬ Subliminal file-Self ▬▬▬▬▬ │
│ You are a nice person               │
│ You are a winner                    │
│ You can be anything you like        │
│ You are smart                       │
│ You are successful                  │
│ You can do it                       │
│ You are wonderful                   │
│ You can have anything               │
│ You will succeed                    │
└─────────────────────────────────────┘
```

Figure 26: *You can view and edit Subliminal files by using any program that saves files in "text" format (Apple's TeachText is shown).*

One last thing: If you get a message that says "Subliminal is not currently installed. Please Restart to install Subliminal," you may not have enough memory available. Try moving one or more extensions or control panels out of your Extensions and Control Panels folders, then restarting your Mac.

SUGGESTIONS FOR USING SUBLIMINAL

Here's one I'd try if I had a boss: First, use a word processor or TeachText to open the file named Subliminal file—Boss. Change "Your Name Here" to your name. (See Figure 27.) If there are special messages you want your boss to see, type them in. Save the file. (Remember, if you used your word processor, save the file in text format only.) Now wait for a time when you and the boss's Mac can be alone together for about five minutes. Copy the Subliminal file—Boss and the Subliminal control panel to a floppy, then copy them into your boss's System Folder and restart the Mac. In the Subliminal control panel, use the Choose File button to select Subliminal file—Boss. Set "Appear every" to 10 minutes and "Display for" to 2 seconds (to make absolutely sure he or she sees the messages). Now scram.

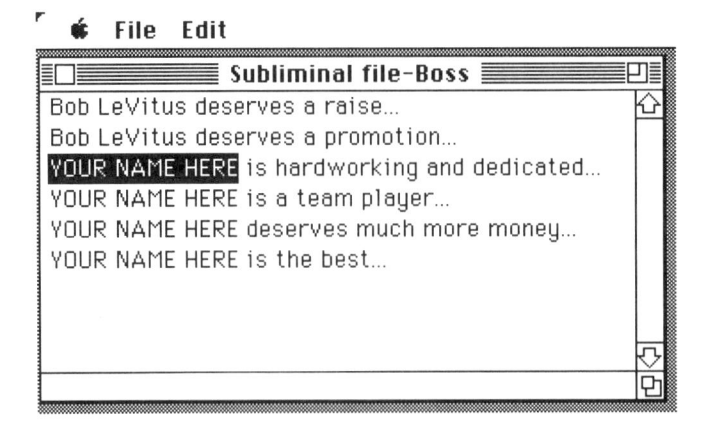

```
 ┌──────────────────────────────────┐
 │  ₡ File  Edit                    │
 ├══════ Subliminal file-Boss ══════┤
 │ Bob LeVitus deserves a raise...  │
 │ Bob LeVitus deserves a promotion.│
 │ YOUR NAME HERE is hardworking and dedicated... │
 │ YOUR NAME HERE is a team player... │
 │ YOUR NAME HERE deserves much more money... │
 │ YOUR NAME HERE is the best...    │
 └──────────────────────────────────┘
```

Figure 27: *Change "Your Name Here" to your name, save the file, and away you go!*

By the end of the day, your boss will give you anything you like as long as you promise you'll make the messages stop!

As you might expect, I don't recommend trying this on a boss with no sense of humor. And of course I can't be held responsible for the consequences.

There are plenty of ways to use Subliminal. It's a wonderful way to suggest things to your spouse. Try: "Wouldn't a new Porsche look good in our garage?" or "Hawaii is nice this time of year." Kids, get anything you want from your parents. Try: "Jacob deserves a much bigger allowance." "Allison would be safer if she had a new car." Parents, use it to reinforce the rules. Try: "Home past midnight = grounded for a month" or "You will do all your chores, or else."

Use your imagination. Remember, even at the fastest setting, one second, you can read most messages. So your so-called subliminal messages are almost certain to be seen. There must be hundreds of other things you can do with it. Go wild.

SUBLIMINAL: THE FINE PRINT

Subliminal © 1991 by Bob LeVitus. Designed and programmed by Evan (Thunder 7) Gross. FreeWare.

LINER NOTES

Subliminal is a Stupid Classic from *Son of Stupid Mac Tricks*. Although the phenomenal Evan Gross programmed it, it was my idea. I'm still pretty proud of it. It's pretty darn stupid, even if I do say so myself.

Over the years, I've received more fan mail for Subliminal than any other trick in any of the Stupid books so far. Why? I have no idea.

Maybe, just maybe, that's because it actually does work. Or not. You be the judge…

TAPPYTYPE

The Macs Are Alive, with the Sound of Typing!

WHAT TAPPYTYPE DOES

Ever long to hear the almost extinct clickety-clack sound of an old manual typewriter? If so, TappyType is just what the doctor (Dr. Macintosh, I presume) ordered! TappyType is a control panel that makes any Mac sound JUST like a manual typewriter. Press any letter or number on the keyboard and hear the distinctive sound of a key striking a platen. Press return and hear the familiar "ding-whoosh" of a carriage returning. Even the space bar makes a proper "manual typewriter" sound. Your Mac has never sounded so fine!

How to Use TappyType

TappyType is a control panel. To activate it, move the TappyType icon onto your System Folder. You'll see the old "Control panels need to be stored in the Control Panels folder..." dialog box. Click OK, then restart your Mac.

TappyType will automatically be placed in the Control Panels folder within your System Folder. To use TappyType, open the Control Panels folder (it's in the System Folder), then open TappyType. (See Figure 28.)

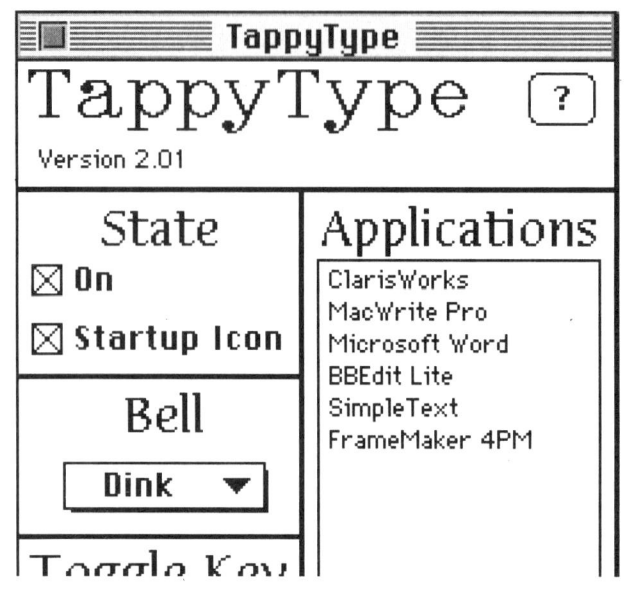

Figure 28: *The TappyType control panel; add your favorite application to the list on the right, then enjoy the melodious tones of an old Underwood.*

TappyType works only in the applications you install in the Application list. It comes with ClarisWorks, MacWrite Pro, Microsoft Word, BBEdit Lite, and SimpleText preinstalled. To add other applications, click the Add button and use the standard Open File dialog box to locate the application on your hard disk. Once it's on the list, TappyType will click and clack every time you use that program.

Click the On checkbox in the TappyType control panel to turn TappyType on or off. If the TappyType control panel is closed, you can use the Toggle Key (preset to Command-Option-T) to turn it on and off. Press Command-Option-T once and it turns off, press it again to turn TappyType back on.

If the Toggle Key conflicts with something in one of your programs, you can change it by opening the TappyType control panel, pressing the Change button, and typing a new Toggle Key.

Suggestions for Using TappyType

I don't know about you, but TappyType is one of a very few Stupid Mac Tricks I can tolerate for more than a few minutes. It reminds me of the good old days. (Yeah, right—those old typewriters didn't have an Undo command or any of the modern conveniences we're so used to.) What I like best is that TappyType gives you the best of both worlds: the sound of an old manual typewriter running on the best personal computer ever made.

It's also lots of fun (and totally harmless) to install on a friend's or boss's computer....

TappyType: Fine Print

TappyType © Colin Klipsch 1989–1995. FreeWare.

Liner Notes

TappyType is a new stupid Mac trick but, like the other new stupid tricks, has been popular on line and around the Internet for years.

Note: Version 2.01, the one on your disk, is more robust and cleaner than its adolescent predecessor, version 1, which was almost included in *Son of Stupid Mac Tricks* but wasn't quite up to snuff back then. Version 2.01 clearly is. Nice work, Colin.

KEY LIGHTS

The Wacky Treat for Your Keyboard's Lights

WHAT KEY LIGHTS DOES

You want to talk about stupid tricks; Key Lights makes the num lock, caps lock, and scroll lock lights on Apple Extended Keyboards flash. You can set the speed and direction of the flashing and create an exceptionally stupid light show on your keyboard.

As far as I know, Key Lights works with Apple-brand Extended Keyboards—the ones with the little lights in the upper-right-hand corner. It may work with other brands, but it may not.

HOW TO USE KEY LIGHTS

Key Lights is a control panel. To activate it, open the Key Lights folder, then drag the Key Lights icon onto your System Folder. You'll see the old "Control panels need to be stored in the Control Panels folder…" dialog box. Click OK, then restart your Mac.

Once you've restarted, Key Lights will be turned on and will create a light show without any further interaction on your part. But the lights are configurable; if you want to change their direction, speed, or normal/inverseness, use the Key Lights control panel.

To configure Key Lights, select Control Panels from the Apple menu and then double-click the Key Lights icon.

Figure 29: *The Key Lights control panel lets you control a light show with the otherwise inert num lock, caps lock, and scroll lock lights on your Apple Extended Keyboard.*

Suggestions for Using Key Lights

Of course, you can run Key Lights on your own Mac to amaze, amuse, and tickle the fancy of all who sit at your desk. It's also sort of fun to install it on other people's Macs. They'll see the little lights blinking, but chances are they won't have a clue as to why.

Key Lights: The Fine Print

Key Lights by Rick Kaseguma © 1990. FreeWare

LINER NOTES

Key Lights is a Stupid Classic from *Son of Stupid Mac Tricks*. It's included here for several reasons, not the least of which is that it takes up very little disk space. It's also the only trick that actually does something to your hardware, a feat worthy of any book with the word *Stupid* in its title. But mostly it's included here 'cause it's really, really dumb.

Bunch o' Icons
A Bevy of Delectable and Delightful Icons (Plus Some Nifty Desktop Patterns!)

What Icons and Desktop Patterns Do

Icons are, well, icons. What's an icon? All the little pictograms we click on to open documents, programs, and folders are icons. Your hard disk, whatever its name, is also an icon.

Icons have been popular since System 7 was introduced several years ago, because System 7 let you move icons from one item to another with great ease (earlier versions of the OS didn't). It's amazing how popular icons are. Log onto any online service and you'll find literally thousands upon thousands of clever icons for your downloading pleasure.

So take a gander at the treasures contained in the the folder Bunch o' Icons. You'll find a wonderful icon starter set with almost 100 beautifully hand-drawn icons for decorating your Macintosh or Mac OS compatible. (See Figure 30.)

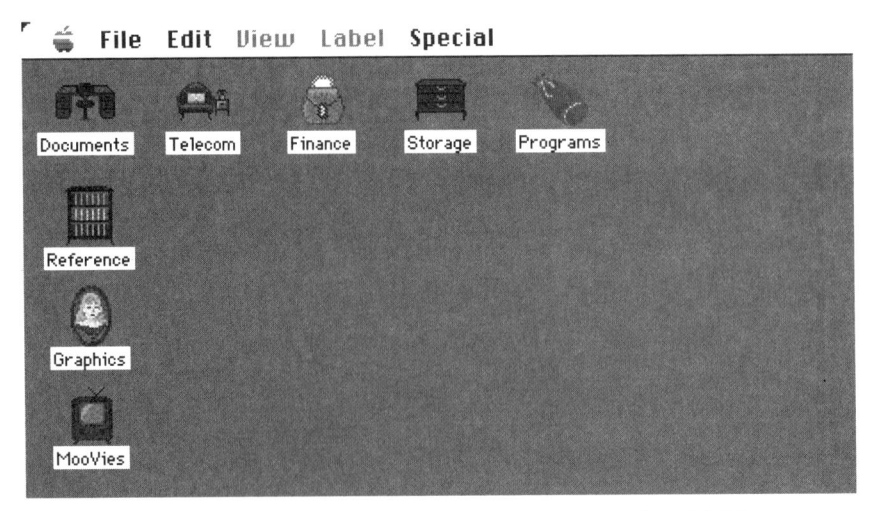

Figure 30: *Give your Mac a makeover with these fanciful icons....*

As a bonus, there's a Desktop Patterns folder inside the Bunch o' Icons folder. Desktop Patterns are another nifty way to redecorate your Mac and turn your boring gray desktop into a beautiful quilt of color (Desktop Patterns require System 7.5). (See Figure 31.)

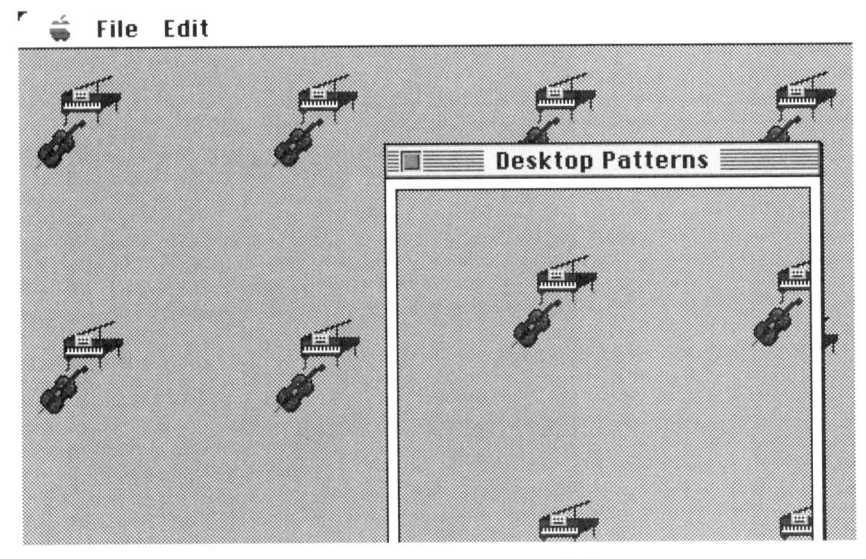

Figure 31: *Desktop Patterns wash the gray right away....*

How To Use Icons And Desktop Patterns

Icons are easy to use. Anything that has an icon can have a different icon if you choose. It's as easy as Copy and Paste. Here's how:

1. Choose an icon you like. Select it by clicking on it once. It should look like the icon Grill in Figure 32.

2. Choose Get Info from the File menu. (See Figure 32.) Or use the power user keyboard shortcut, Command-I.

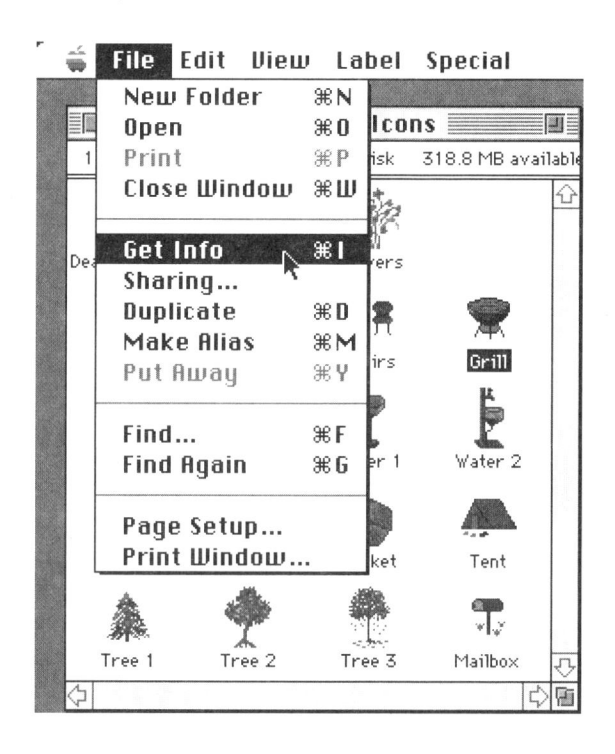

Figure 32: *Select an icon you like; then choose Get Info from the File menu.*

3. Now click directly on the picture of the grill in the upper-left corner of the Get Info window. (See Figure 33.)

Figure 33: *Click directly on the icon (left). If you do it correctly, a box will appear around it (right).*

4. Choose Copy from the Edit menu.

5. Find the icon you want to receive the makeover. Select it by single-clicking it. It's called Make me a Grill! in Figure 34.

6. Choose Get Info from the File menu. Click directly on the picture in the upper-left corner of the Get Info window. A square should appear around the icon. Choose Paste from the Edit menu. (See Figure 34.) The result is shown in Figure 35.

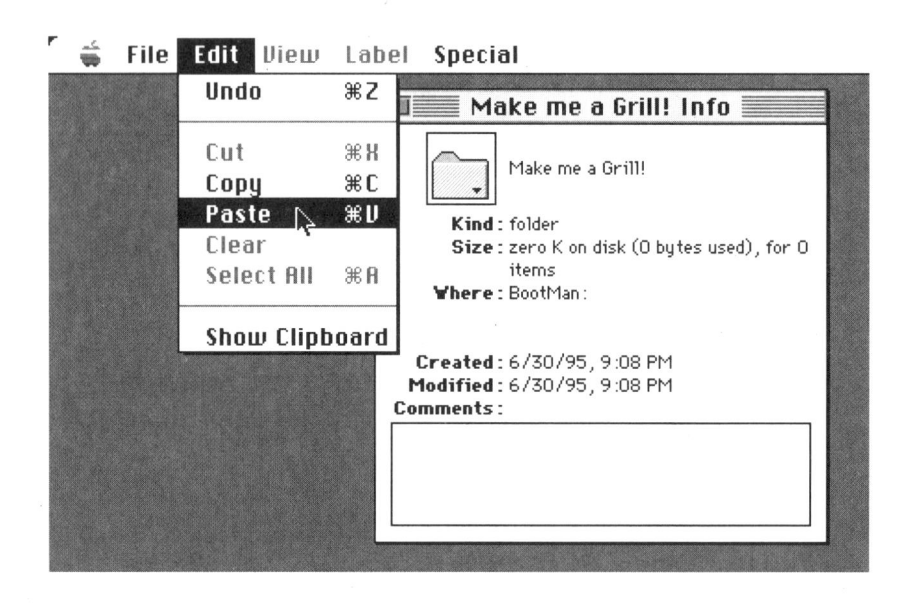

Figure 34: *The folder Make me a Grill! is about to have its wish granted.*

```
╔══════════════════════════╗
║ ▣ ═ Make me a Grill! Info ═ ║
╟──────────────────────────╢
║  [grill]  Make me a Grill!  ║
║                          ║
║   Kind: folder           ║
║   Size: zero K on disk (0 bytes used), for 0
║         items            ║
║  Where: BootMan:         ║
╚══════════════════════════╝
```

Figure 35: *After pasting, the folder icon disappears, replaced by the grill icon.*

That's all there is to icons: Select, Get Info, Click, Copy; Select, Get Info, Click, Paste. Piece of cake. I'll wait here while you play with them for a while.

There's just one last thing you should know about icons. To get an icon back the way it was, merely click it once to select it, Get Info (File menu, remember?), click the icon in the Get Info window, then press the Delete key on your keyboard.

Desktop Patterns are another way to dress up your Mac. As I mentioned, they require System 7.5. If you have System 7.5, you're in for a treat. Open the Control Panels folder, then open Desktop Patterns. Next, open the MyDesktop folder (inside the Bunch o' Icons folder, which is inside the N & I Stupid Mac Tricks Folder, which you should have installed a long time ago.)

Now click on one of the desktop patterns—Living desk, Den desk, Music desk, etc.—and drag it right onto the Desktop Patterns control panel. (See Figure 36.)

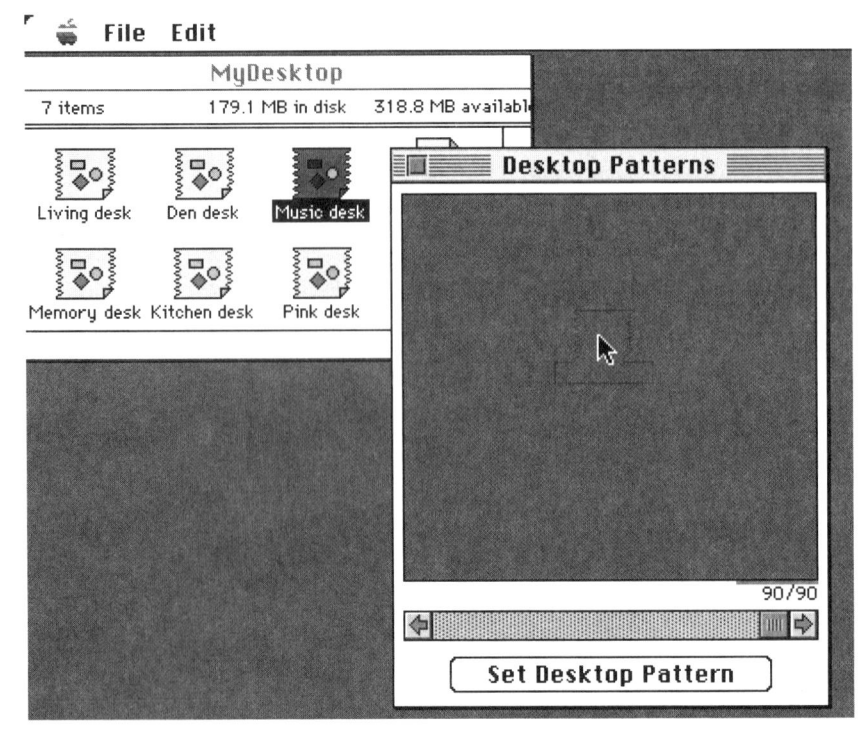

Figure 36: *Drag the icon right onto the Desktop Patterns window.*

Release the mouse button when the icon is in the middle of the Desktop Patterns window, as shown in Figure 36. When you release the mouse button, click the Set Desktop Pattern button to make that desktop pattern your own.

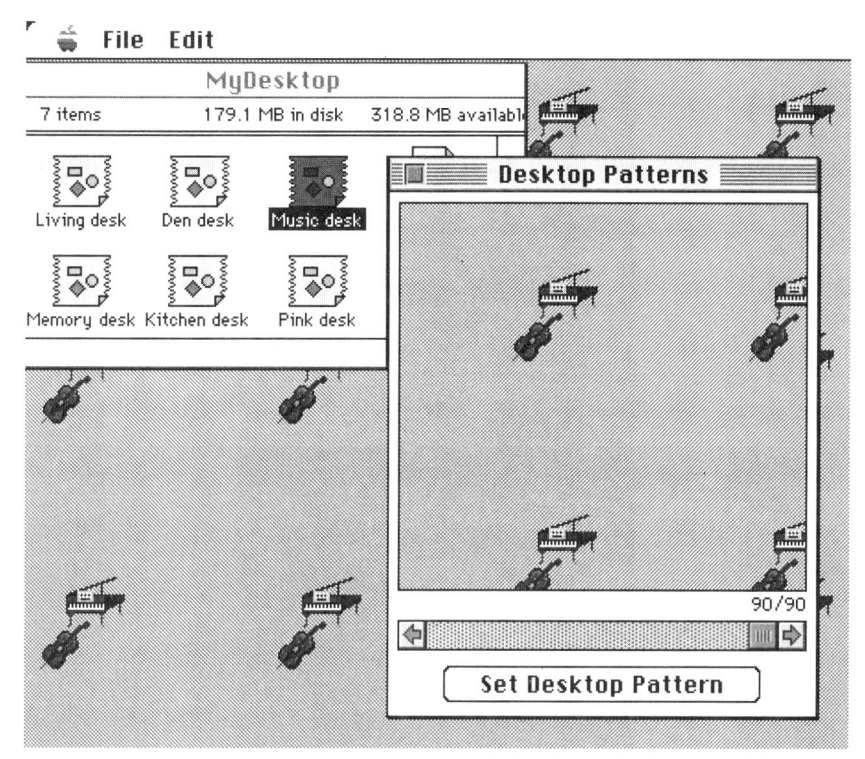

Figure 37: *Click the Set Desktop Pattern button and banish your gray desktop forever!*

SUGGESTIONS FOR USING ICONS AND DESKTOP PATTERNS

Duh. Go crazy. Redecorate your Mac. Have fun!

Icons and Desktop Patterns: Fine Print

MyRoom, MyRoom#2, MyBags, and MyBackyard icons, by Sachiko Oba (sachi@interport.net). MyDesktop desktop patterns are also by Sachiko. If you like them, please send her comments. The Macintosh Icons are by George Stolz. He'd like you to send him $5; if you do, he'll send you 50 more icons (see the Read Me file).

Liner Notes

Icons and Desktop Patterns are new to *Stupid Mac Tricks* books. That's mostly because they weren't possible with earlier versions of the operating system.

Ain't progress grand? Sachiko's icons are among the sweetest I've seen; George's Mac icons are stupider but still worth having.

If you like these icons and desktop patterns and have a modem, zillions more can be found on CompuServe, America Online, the Internet, and other online playgrounds in your neck of cyberspace.

Sexist Mac Tricks
Sexplosion, Babe-o-Rama, and Jiggling Jugs

Disclaimer and Obligatory Warning Text

The stupid tricks in the "Sexist Mac Tricks" section (and folder on your hard disk) have names and icons that are truly sexist. I apologize for that, but the names and icons weren't my idea. I think you'll find that the tricks themselves are pretty funny—or, at the very least, pretty stupid! So at the behest of my publisher, here's the obligatory warning:

WARNING: If material of a frank and sexual nature offends you, DO NOT LOOK at the tricks in the Sexist Mac Tricks folder, and DO NOT READ the next three sections.

Of course, as you'll discover if you choose to explore Sexist Mac Tricks, there's actually nothing of a frank and sexual nature about them (except, perhaps, if you are particularly puritanical, their icons and names.) Even there you'll see nothing you couldn't see on daytime network television. Still, they are clearly sexist, and I feel better having warned you.

My recommendation is to ignore the obnoxious names and icons. If you can, I think you'll find Sexplosion, Babe-O-Rama, and Jiggling Jugs among the stupidest Mac tricks you've seen.

SEXPLOSION
It's Not What You Expect...

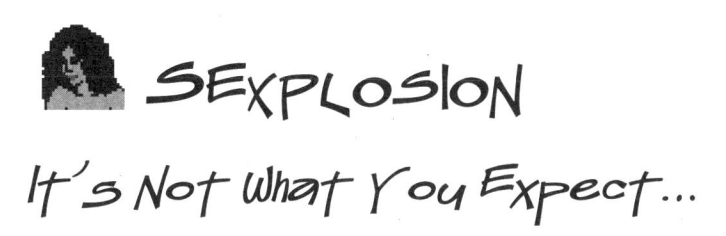

WHAT SEXPLOSION DOES

When you start Sexplosion by double-clicking its suggestive icon, it bombs. Or at least it appears to bomb. (See Figure 38.)

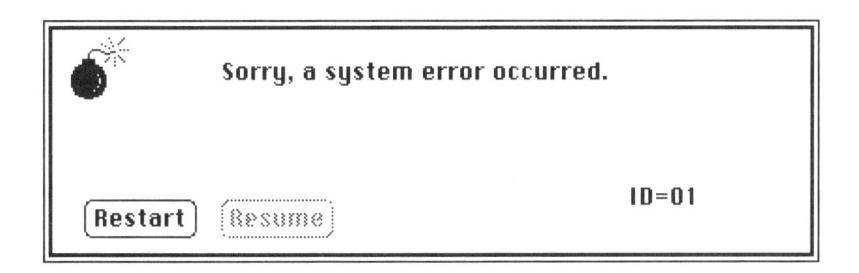

Figure 38: *Double-clicking the suggestive Sexplosion icon brings up this phony-baloney "bomb" dialog box.*

But this bomb is a bomb with a difference. You see, when you try to click Sexplosion's Restart button, the button squirms out from under your cursor—a frustrating and unique sensory experience. (See Figure 39.)

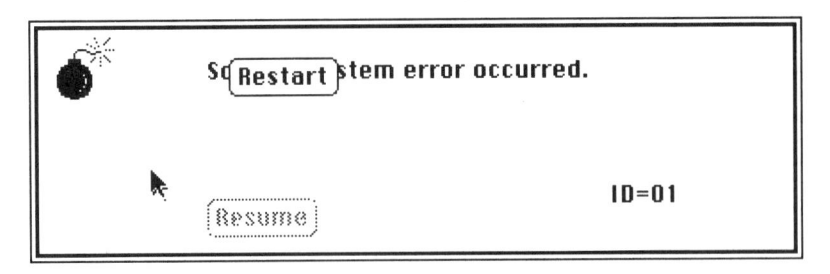

Figure 39: *When you try to click the Restart button, Sexplosion stubbornly refuses to let you—the button squirms away from the cursor!*

How to Use Sexplosion

Sexplosion is an application. Just double-click its suggestive icon to bring up the bomb dialog box.

The secret of Sexplosion (and the only thing you need to know) is that to quit, you click on the grayed-out Resume button, not the squirming Restart button. Simple, eh? Your friends won't think so!

Suggestions for Using Sexplosion

When I'm showing off stuff my Mac can do, I almost always open the folder that contains Sexplosion. (I call the folder "X-RATED—KEEP OUT" for effect!) Almost everybody asks, "What is that?" I move away and say "Double-click it—it's really neat!" When the bomb dialog box appears, I pretend to be surprised and say "Oh, darn. I don't know why that thing is bombing. Click the Restart button and we'll try it again." Then I sit back and giggle as the would-be bomber tries to click the moving button, a physical impossibility. Finally, I click the grayed-out Resume button and end the person's agony.

This is a dangerous trick to put on someone else's Mac, and I don't recommend you do so. He or she might think it's a real bomb and restart the Mac by shutting off the power, which could cause a loss of data. Someone using System 7 or later and having unsaved work in an open application could lose it. I urge you to be responsible with Sexplosion. Don't just leave it on someone's machine without revealing its secret.

Sexplosion: Fine Print

Sexplosion! v 1.0. © 1987–1990 by Bob Schumaker. Click the bomb icon to see complete credits. All rights reserved. HappiWare—if you like it, SMILE!

Liner Notes

Sexplosion is a Stupid Classic from *Stupid Mac Tricks*.

Sexplosion is based on one of the oldest Stupid Tricks I know, one known, at various times in its life, as Bomber or Hot Sex. They worked almost exactly like our Sexplosion but were not 100% MultiFinder (the predecessor to System 7) compatible and left traces of themselves on screen after they were closed. Since I couldn't find the author of Bomber/Hot Sex to ask him or her to fix this problem, I asked my good buddy and ace programmer Bob Schumaker if he could create something similar-but-well-behaved-under-MultiFinder for my the original Stupid Mac Tricks (circa 1990). Sexplosion is what he came up with. And it's still as funny as it was almost 6 years ago.

Nice work, Bob. Thanks again.

BABE-O-RAMA
It's DEFINITELY Not What You Expect...

WHAT BABE-O-RAMA DOES

When you start Babe-O-Rama by double-clicking its suggestive icon, it does something completely unexpected.... (See Figure 40.)

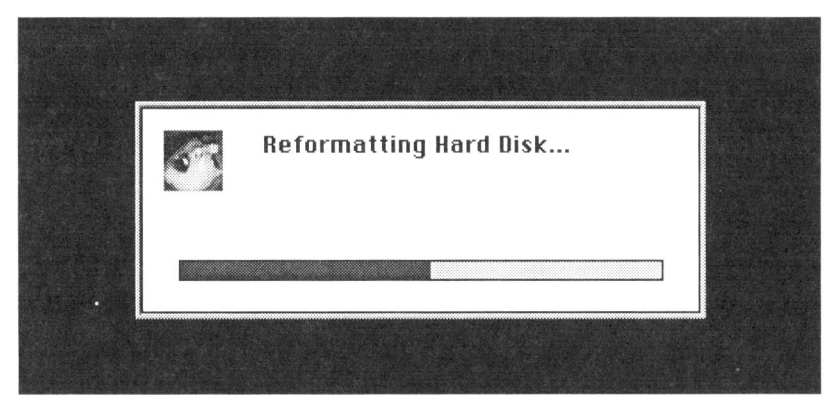

Figure 40: *Pretty scary, eh? Just remember, it's only a joke.*

How to Use Babe-o-Rama

Babe-O-Rama (we'll call it BOR) is an application. Just double-click its suggestive icon to start the fun. Once you launch it, BOR emits a scary sound, then tells you it's "Preparing to Reformat Hard Disk." Next, you see a realistic-looking dialog box that looks like it's reformatting your hard disk, as shown in Figure 40. After a few seconds the dialog box says, "Ha, Ha, Ha...," then, "Just Kidding." Finally, you see another dialog box informing you that you are a victim of a CyByrSoft Gag. (See Figure 41.)

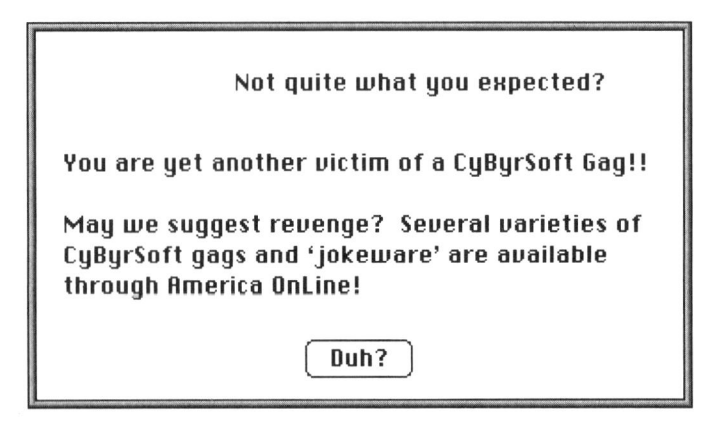

```
Not quite what you expected?

You are yet another victim of a CyByrSoft Gag!!

May we suggest revenge? Several varieties of
CyByrSoft gags and 'jokeware' are available
through America OnLine!

[ Duh? ]
```

Figure 41: *The last thing Babe-O-Rama does before it quits automatically, is to admit it was only a joke.*

Suggestions for Using Babe-o-Rama

Of course, you can leave BOR on your own desktop. If someone happens to double-click it, don't forget to scream at the top of your lungs, "OH NO!! Don't do THAT!"

Like Sexplosion, BOR is a dangerous trick to put on other people's Macs, and I don't recommend you do so. They might think it's really reformatting their hard disk and restart their Macs by shutting off the power, which could lead to data loss. If they're using System 7 or later and have unsaved work in an open application, they could lose it. I urge you to be responsible with BOR. Don't just leave it on someone's machine; stick around to prevent him or her from doing anything really stupid.

Fine Print: Babe-O-Rama

Babe-O-Rama © Brian Cyr, 1994. FreeWare.

Liner Notes

Babe-O-Rama is a new Stupid Mac Trick, but it's been popular on the Internet and online services since its introduction. Brian Cyr's other jokeware, including Jiggling Jugs (see next section) can be found on most online services and the Internet.

JIGGLING JUGS

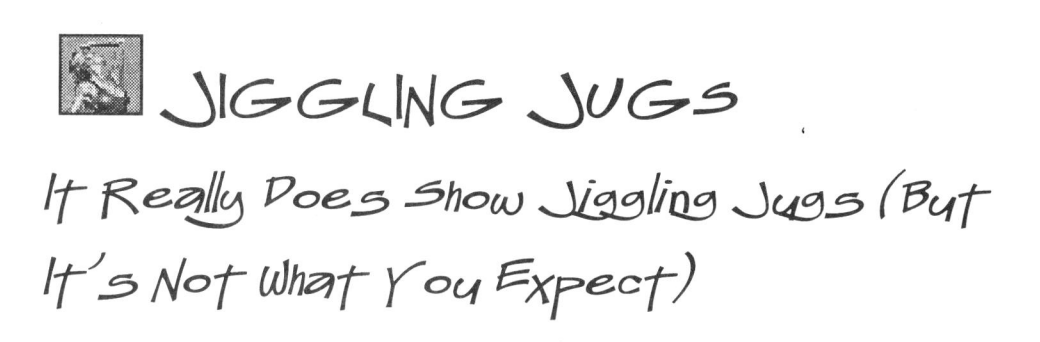

It Really Does Show Jiggling Jugs (But It's Not What You Expect)

WHAT JIGGLING JUGS DOES

When you start Jiggling Jugs by double-clicking its suggestive icon, it does exactly what you expect—it displays a pair of jiggling jugs. (See Figure 42.)

Figure 42: *Launch Jiggling Jugs and you'll see (what did you expect?) a pair of life-sized jugs, jiggling.*

How to Use Jiggling Jugs

Jiggling Jugs is an application. Just double-click its suggestive icon to start the fun. Once you launch it, a realistic-looking dialog box informs you that Jiggling Jugs is intended for mature viewing audiences only. (See Figure 43.)

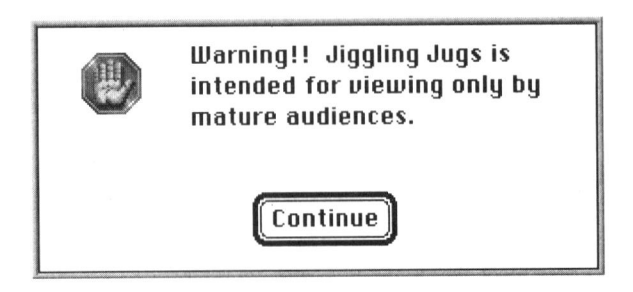

Figure 43: *You're warned before the Jugs appear.*

If you click the Continue button, you'll be treated to a pair of jugs, jiggling energetically, as seen in Figure 42. Click anywhere on screen to quit the program (before it quits, you'll see a familiar dialog box, the same as the one in Figure 41.)

Suggestions for Using Jiggling Jugs

Of course, you can leave Jiggling Jugs on your own desktop. Someone who happens to double-click it will get only what he or she deserves.

Unlike Sexplosion and BOR, Jiggling Jugs is totally harmless, making it a lot of fun to put on someone else's Mac.

If you have electronic mail, Jiggling Jugs is a pretty small program (less than 60K), so it's easy to send to your friends. Try to imagine the look (disappointment?) on their faces when they try it.

FINE PRINT: BABE-O-RAMA

Jiggling Jugs © Brian Cyr, 1994. FreeWare

LINER NOTES

Jiggling Jugs is a new Stupid Mac Trick, but, like its spiritual sibling Babe-O-Rama, it's been popular on the Internet and online services since its introduction. Brian Cyr's other jokeware, including Babe-O-Rama (see previous section) can be found on most online services and the Internet.

Glossary
Daffy-Nitions

Application (a.k.a. Program)

Applications are programs; they run when you double-click their icon. Shakespeare, EyeCon, and all the Sexist tricks are applications.

Control Panel

A file you activate by dragging it onto your System Folder and restarting your Mac. Control panels live in the Control Panels folder inside the System Folder. To use them, open the Control Panels folder and double-click them.

Holding down the Shift key at startup tells your Mac to not load ANY control panels or extensions. To deactivate a control panel, move it out of the Control Panels folder and into any folder except the System Folder, or drag it into the Trash, then restart your Mac.

Blood, EarthQuake, Key Lights, Subliminal, Tappy-Type, and UnderWare Demo are control panels.

Commercial Software

Software sold by publishers. Commercial software may not be copied or given away. Examples: Microsoft Word, Adobe PageMaker.

See also Freeware; Shareware.

Desk Accessory (a.k.a. DA)

Special miniprograms available in the Apple menu (System 6 or 7) or by double-clicking their icon (System 7 only).

Desk accessories are becoming rarer. Melt is the only desk accessory in the collection.

Finder

A special file, part of your necessary System software, that manages opening, closing, moving, naming, trashing files and folders, and mounting and ejecting disks. The Finder runs automatically whenever you start up your Mac and is responsible for managing the desktop you see when you turn on your Mac. You must have, at the very least, a System and a Finder on any disk used to start up your Mac, and the System and Finder files must always be in a special folder that must be named the System Folder.

Freeware

Software for which there is no charge and that can be copied and given away freely. This does not necessarily mean that the program is "in the public domain." An author *may* still retain all rights to his/her software even though allowing it to be distributed freely.

Extension

A file you activate by dragging it into your System Folder and restarting your Mac. Extensions live in the Extensions folder inside the System Folder. They have no user-adjustable controls. If they're in your Extensions folder (and you're not holding down the Shift key), they load at startup.

Holding down the Shift key at startup tells your Mac to not load ANY extensions or control panels.

To deactivate an extension, move it out of the Extensions folder and into any folder except the System Folder, or drag it into the Trash, then restart your Mac.

Belch!, Critters, and Enchanted Menus are all Mac extensions.

Online Service

A large, commercial BBS (bulletin board system). Online services let computer users who have modems upload and download text and programs and leave messages for other users. You can also shop for a wide variety of products, buy and sell stocks, make travel reservations, and search huge electronic databases for specific information. Fees average from $2 to $20 an hour.

I first saw most of the tricks in this book after

downloading them from an online service. CompuServe and America Online are the most popular online services for Macintosh users.

Read Me File (a.k.a. Doc File)

A text file that comes with other software. Whenever you see a Read Me or Doc file in a folder, you should read it before you proceed. If you double-click one and get a message that says "An application can't be found for this document," launch your word processor (or the SimpleText application that comes on most Apple System Software disks) and use its Open command to open the Read Me file.

Shareware

Try-before-you-buy software. May be copied and given out freely, but if you use it regularly, you are honor-bound to send some money to the author. In some cases (Macintosh Icons) you get extra stuff if you send money. In other cases (EarthQuake), you get nothing more than the peace of mind that comes from doing the right thing. Those are the only two ShareWare programs in this collection—all the rest are FreeWare.

System 6

An earlier, less capable version of Macintosh Operating System.

System 7 (System 7.x)

The current version of the Macintosh OS. (Actually, System 7.5.1 is the current version.)

Since there are numerous versions of System 7 (7.0.1, 7.1, 7.5, 7.5.1, etc.), we use the designation 7.x to refer to them collectively.

User Group (a.k.a. MUG—Macintosh User Group)

A club made up of Macintosh enthusiasts. There are more than 1000 such clubs in North America. Most hold regular meetings and classes, publish a newsletter, obtain discounts on goods and services, and maintain shareware/freeware libraries for their members. To find the user group nearest you, call (800) 538-9696, ext. 500.

About the Disk

The enclosed disk brings you 17 of the funniest, most stupid tricks Bob LeVitus has run into recently, which you can load on your Mac, or someone else's if you're the sneaky type. They all work with System 7 and later (through 7.5) and any Mac can run them (including Power Macs).

System Requirements

A Macintosh, a hard disk drive, a high density floppy disk drive, and Macintosh Operating System Software version 7.0 or later. A color monitor is recommended, but not essential for the enjoyment of most tricks.